Joe Stahlkuppe

Poodles

Everything about Purchase, Care, Nutrition,
Breeding, Behavior, and Training

With 41 Color Photographs

Illustrations by Michele Earle-Bridges

BARRON'S

About the Author

Joe Stahlkuppe, a lifelong dog fancier and breeder, writes dog columns for several pet and general interest publications. A former U.S. Army journalist in Vietnam and teacher, he is also the author of Barron's *Irish Setters: A Complete Pet Owner's Manual, Great Danes: A Complete Pet Owner's Manual,* and *American Pit Bull and Staffordshire Terriers: A Complete Pet Owner's Manual.* Mr. Stahlkuppe lives with his wife, Cathie, on a small farm in Alabama and looks forward to teaching his granddaughter Ann Catherine about dogs.

Photo Credits

Paulette Braun: front cover, back cover, pages 12, 13 top, 13 bottom, 17, 37, 81, 100 bottom; Barbara Augello: inside front cover, pages 9 bottom, 45, 84; Bob Schwartz: inside back cover, pages 20 top, 20 bottom, 24, 28 top, 33, 36, 40, 41, 44, 53, 60, 88, 89, 97; Susan Green: contents page, pages 28 bottom, 29, 52, 69; Toni Tucker: pages 8, 9 top; Judith Strom: pages 21, 61, 68, 100 top; Michele Earle-Bridges: page 32; Jean Wentworth: page 57.

All inquiries should be addressed to:
Barron's Educational Series, Inc.
250 Wireless Boulevard
Hauppauge, NY 11788

International Standard Book No. 0-8120-9738-6

Library of Congress Catalog Card No. 96-28312

Library of Congress Cataloging-in-Publication Data
Stahlkuppe, Joe.
    Poodles : everything about purchase, care, nutrition, breeding, behavior, and training / Joe Stahlkuppe ; illustrations by Michele Earle-Bridges.
        p.   cm.—(A Complete pet owner's manual)
    Includes bibliographical references and index.
    ISBN 0-8120-9738-6
    1. Poodles. I. Title. II. Series.
SF429.P85S67   1997
636.7′2—dc20   96-28312
                                                  CIP

Printed in Hong Kong

19 18 17 16 15 14 13 12 11 10

Important Note

This pet owner's guide tells the reader how to buy and care for a poodle. The author and the publisher consider it important to point out that the advice given in the book is meant primarily for normally developed puppies from a good breeder—that is, dogs of excellent physical health and good character.

Anyone who adopts a fully grown dog should be aware that the animal has already formed its basic impressions of human beings. The new owner should watch the animal carefully, including its behavior toward humans, and should meet the previous owner. If the dog comes from a shelter, it may be possible to get some information on the dog's background and peculiarities there. There are dogs that, as a result of bad experiences with humans, behave in an unnatural manner or may even bite. Only people that have experience with dogs should take in such animals.

Caution is further advised in the association of children with dogs, in meeting with other dogs, and in exercising the dog without a leash.

Even well-behaved and carefully supervised dogs sometimes do damage to someone else's property or cause accidents. It is therefore in the owner's interest to be adequately insured against such eventualities, and we strongly urge all dog owners to purchase a liability policy that covers their dog.

Contents

The toy poodle (left), should be the same in all aspects as the miniature poodle (center), which should be the same in all aspects as the standard poodle (right), except for the obvious size differences.

Preface

This book is aimed at first-time poodle owners and at those who think they might want to be first-time poodle owners. Poodles offer a great deal to novice and experienced dog owners alike. If you go about selecting the right poodle in the right way, you have a good chance at success!

The poodle is in a crisis today, a crisis brought about by popularity and overbreeding, and the consequences of both. The Poodle Club of America has valiantly battled to undo all the effects of the breed's celebrity status. Rescue efforts, under the able leadership of Helen Taylor, have saved countless poodles from certain death or uncertain life. Research funded by the PCA will some day find answers to some of the medical dilemmas facing the poodle of today. Responsible poodle breeders everywhere are tightening up the requirements they set for just who can and who cannot obtain a poodle puppy.

Any other breed would have wilted under the intense scrutiny, the false public image, the myriad of genetic pitfalls, and the greed-driven efforts of the puppy factory crowd. Any other breed would have put its pompon between its legs and slinked away to oblivion. Any other breed might have done that, but the poodle is not any other breed!

This book is respectfully dedicated to the members of the Poodle Club of America who have:

1. Refused to let public opinion sway them in their quest to save the poodle.

2. Refused to let a pantheon of medical problems sink the poodle.

3. Refused to let the mass producers of poorly bred poodle puppies get away with it.

4. Refused to let the stylish set turn the poodle into a fashion accessory.

I want to thank Barron's for its patience with this book, especially Amanda Pisani, a newcomer editor who handled the project like a veteran. Michele Earle-Bridges deserves high praise for her creative talent as an illustrator and as a person. Nancy Hafner of Alabama and Helen Taylor of Texas are two poodle breeders who have been extremely helpful in the writing of this book.

Special thanks go to a remarkable writer and dedicated dog person, Sharon Pflaumer, who captured the essence of this breed in a well-written article in *Dog World Magazine*. That magazine's managing editor, Kim Dearth, helped in several important areas.

Cathie, my wife, deserves a medal for her help with this and several other books. My son Shawn and daughter-in-law Lisa made it possible for my granddaughter Ann Catherine to be around to see this book. Thanks also to three friends: Leon Frazier, John Tadlock, and Guy Moore.

Note: The dog on page 60 is a miniature poodle!

Poodles:
An Introduction

Everyone knows the "French" poodle, don't they? Not necessarily! One of the most popular breeds in the world, poodles have often been cursed by the misconceptions that such popularity can bring. People have neatly filed the concept of "poodle" into classifications of superfluous, dandified, even useless as a *real* dog. This is far from the truth!

Derivation of the Name

The poodle is the national dog of France, but the breed isn't actually French. The dogs we know as poodles (which the French call *caniches*)

The stylish poodle of today got its start in the bays, rivers, and marshes of Europe as the best waterfowl retriever of its time.

come from early German retrievers, which came to be called *pudels,* taking their name from an Old German word for "puddler" or "to splash in or into water." Caniche, the French name for their adopted favorite, comes from the word *canard*, or duck, making the caniche a "duck dog." Thus, in both their home country and in their adoptive land, poodles are known, by name, for their ability to retrieve downed ducks or geese for hunters.

The Origin of the Poodle Clip

This early poodle was a stockier version of the standard or large poodle of today. What many experts believe was a fortunate mutation gave these tough retrievers a dense and tightly curled coat that made cold water retrieving less chilling. Even the haircuts or clips that have contributed so much to the impression of the poodle as a dandy, or a pampered pet, originated with hunters. Even before the 1300s, duck hunters began trimming away some of the poodle's heavy coat to assist the dog in swimming after downed waterfowl in rough water. Thus, the easily recognized "lion clip," which left poodles with a full mane in front and shaved hindquarters, began as an effort by duck and goose hunters to cover the areas of the retrieving poodles that would be most sensitive to cold, while freeing up the rear of the dog to aid it in swimming. The puffs of hair left on the legs were not decoration but insulation to protect the dogs' joints from cold water. The oft-ridiculed pompon on the dogs' three-quarter-length tail was left to serve as a type of rudder. It also made a useful signal flag that let hunters know the location of their dogs in choppy, rolling waters.

Poodles' Functions

The poodle is one of the oldest distinct dog breeds. From the first century, Greek carvings depicted dogs that greatly resemble poodles. European artwork and texts from the fifteenth century clearly show and describe poodles in a variety of settings from a working "water dog" to a popular pet.

Hunters and Retrievers

As retrievers, early poodles spent a lot of time with humans. Hunting was a very serious endeavor that brought needed food to the table, and lost waterfowl were considered a great waste. Not only did poodles need to be obedient to the hunters' commands, but these dogs also had to be "soft-mouthed" so that they would not tear or bruise the flesh of the ducks or geese they retrieved. Poodles also had to be tough enough to bring in a large duck or goose that was only wounded and that still could put up quite a fight.

Poodles had to be patient as they waited, hidden with their owners. They had to remain motionless in order to not frighten away incoming waterfowl. They had to remain in place until the command to go after their owners' kills was given. Sometimes a poodle would be required to swim long distances, against the current, in turbulent water, towing one or more ducks or a large goose. Obedience, especially to shouted commands and hand signals, was a must.

Poodles could not be quarrelsome with the other hunters' retrievers, but

Poodle clips weren't always for decorative purposes. Originally, retrieving poodles were trimmed to better help them swim. Joints and chest were left untrimmed to insulate them from the effects of icy-cold water.

had to be strong enough and have enough endurance to make repeated retrieves before accompanying the hunter/master on the long walk home. These hard-working dogs had to be able to survive on the sometimes meager fare they shared with their owners. Unlike hounds and other types of hunting dogs that were kept, often in kennels, for the chase or to attack and bring down game, poodles usually became beloved family pets and actually lived with the hunter and his family.

Companions

Poodles served as nursemaids for toddlers, family watchdogs and protectors, and sturdy companions. Sometimes the poodle would have to pull a cart to market for the hunter's wife. Some poodles helped herd cattle and they had to be courageous enough to battle predators intent on killing livestock. Poodles, later viewed by some as soft pet dogs, handled all these chores and more.

Beginning as early as the thirteenth century in Germany, France, and other

The poodle is one of the most popular breeds in the world and this cafe-au-lait miniature seems to be basking in its popularity.

non-hunters, wealthy Europeans, and even royalty. Poodles began to move from the modest, rural homes of waterfowl hunters, to city houses and castles.

By the 1600s, poodles had become regular fixtures in many portraits made of the landed gentry, wealthy merchants, and various royal families. Poodles had to adapt in size in order to fit the needs of their new masters and mistresses. To the standard poodle were gradually added two smaller versions. This was largely accomplished by breeding smaller and smaller poodles together. Decreasing poodle size soon became a major dog-breeding goal. The miniature poodle and the early toy poodle were already known by 1600. The standard poodle continued bringing in waterfowl, but even this largest poodle was becoming more popular as a showy pet.

Note: In Europe today there are *four* poodle sizes: toy, medium, miniature, and standard.

Some smaller poodles became expert "truffle dogs," using their sense of smell to seek and find these tasty underground fungi. Poodles were sometimes teamed with, or even interbred with, basset hounds, dachshunds, or small terriers to find and dig up these subterranean delicacies.

At about this same time—the late fourteenth and early fifteenth centuries—poodles became popular as performers in the traveling shows, circuses, and carnivals that provided much of the entertainment of that era. This role, one that continues for poodles today, helped poodles to become well-known over much of Europe and the British Isles. Seeing poodles in humorous costumes or performing clever tricks helped build wide acceptance of the breed. These circuses and itinerant shows brought poodles before large audiences that had never been involved with duck or goose

parts of Europe, poodles were recognized as the ideal combination of hunters/workers and family dogs. Their long years of closeness to humankind (and their owners' subsequent selective breeding of the smartest, most obedient, and best retrievers) made an indelible mark on the form, structure, and personality of the poodle.

Adaptability

Poodles gained adaptability during the many years that they served as companions. As much as any breed of dog, they were able to adjust to and for people. Adapting came early for poodles, but it also meant filling new and vastly different roles.

Gradually, beginning in the thirteenth or fourteenth century, poodles came to be treasured by more than hunters and their families. Their pet qualities and unique appearance began to attract

hunting and were therefore not familiar with these dogs. Capable and bright, seemingly pleased by the attention and applause, poodles learned a wide range of tricks and routines that amazed and amused their audiences.

Beautiful and Elegant

Poodles are more than mops of curly hair perched on the arm of some socialite or mincing along a boulevard at the end of a leash. Poodles are more than clever performers or statuesque show dogs. Most poodles still show the athletic build of their retriever ancestors. In very harmonious terms, poodles have long legs attached to short bodies with broad, full chests. The head of the poodle is well-shaped and placed atop a fine, but muscular neck. Seen without the solid-colored, tight, curly coat, standard poodles would physically resemble a number of other working bird dogs or water spaniels.

Sizes

Standard poodles, shorn of coat, are actually about the size and overall shape of some of such continental hunting dogs as the Weimaraner, the German shorthaired pointer, or the vizsla. Today's standard poodle is above 15 inches (38 cm) in height at the shoulder (generally well above this limit). The miniature poodle is under 15 inches but above 10 inches (2.5 m) in height at the shoulder. The height, at the shoulder, of a toy poodle must be 10 inches or below (see Standard, page 13).

Coat

The poodle's coat attracted the eye of the dog owner and the dog fancier who fashioned the poodle's natural outerwear by trimming it, clipping it, plucking it, shaping it, and even dying it into a number of dramatic outlines and appearances.

The expression on this standard poodle's face sums up the way that this breed is devoted to its owners. Poodles love their humans with something quite close to worship.

The poodle started out as a rugged retriever of downed waterfowl, a task that this black standard could perform well.

Underneath the poodle's showy exterior is an athletic physique that dates back to when poodles were rugged retrievers.

Another variety of poodle coat, seen in the corded poodle, whose uncut coat falls in rope-like spirals instead of tight curls, was never as popular in the United States as it has been in other parts of the world. The tendency toward a corded coat may be genetically determined as most poodles' coats cannot be corded. Some corded poodles can, however, have their coats reworked into the more recognizable clipped or trimmed types and some can't. Corded poodles once had a breed club of their own, but their popularity has greatly decreased in recent decades.

The Real Dog Inside the Perceived Poodle

The poodle has been relegated by some into the unfortunate status of a living, breathing fashion accessory. This attitude does both the dog and the dog's owner a true disservice. Even in its toy variety, the poodle is much more than an adornment or an ornament. An ornament can be taken off and put away when not in use, but a dog needs consistent care, affection, and attention.

Poodle owners suffer most when they fail to recognize poodles for the versatile dogs they can be. Anyone who purchases a poodle solely for the visual impact the dog will have on passersby is getting a pet, and especially a poodle, for all the wrong reasons! Poodles are very devoted and trusting canines whose pet qualities do not begin and end with their appearance.

Each type of poodle has much to offer as a pet. Standard poodles are still more than capable of becoming solid and dependable retrievers. These larger poodles have served in law enforcement, as guide dogs for the sight-impaired, and astonishingly, as competition for Malamutes and huskies in the most grueling of Alaskan sled dog races—the Iditarod!

Disposition

Well-bred poodles are usually cheerful, confident dogs. They have been associated with humans long enough to fit in well in almost every kind of lifestyle:
• The standard poodle can grace a stroll with its owner in a city park, patrol a suburban backyard, or function in a duck blind.
• The miniature poodle can be a child's best friend, a family's furriest member, or a hardworking obedience trial dog.
• While equally at home in suburban or rural settings, the toy poodle can be just the right dog for the individual or couple bound by space constraints in a small apartment, or for a retiree needing companionship.

Poodles star as therapy dogs, bringing smiles to sick children, happiness to disabled older persons, and unreserved affection to the developmentally disadvantaged. Poodles have proven many times over that a friendly dog can be medicine of a very special kind.

Intelligence

Poodles are quick to learn and slow to forget. Poodle owners *must* learn to be consistent with their dog. A poodle that has been allowed on the couch at one time will not understand being banned from that same couch later. Some poodles react to such inequities with resentment.

Poodles, like their circus-dog ancestors, are usually easy to teach both commands and tricks. They learn from a variety of teachers and learning situations. We know of one young poodle puppy that was brought into a home as a replacement for a very old poodle that did not have long to live. The old dog had a habit of alerting its mistress with a quick bark, immediately after the first ring, whenever the telephone rang. The alert was always one quick bark that the dog's family came to think of as "PePe's telephone bark." The old dog did this a number of times in the presence of the puppy. Some days after the old dog finally died, the telephone rang and the family was astonished when the new poodle pup gave the same single, quick bark it had heard and learned from watching the old pet. The pup continued this practice throughout its life.

The Perfect Dog?

Advocates of many breeds tout them as *perfect* dogs, glossing over breed imperfections and expanding on the good points the breed has to offer. It may be true that some poodle supporters have also taken this position at times. If so, overly enthusiastic poodle fans are just as wrong as any other proponents of any other *perfect* breed.

Is the poodle the perfect breed? Of course not! The poodle, as a breed with three varieties, is beset by some of the most serious genetic health problems in purebred dogs. There are great poodles, but they don't come from casual sources (mass puppy-breeding facilities or haphazard back-yard matings), and they don't come cheap or without responsibilities.

Each size of poodle has its own special needs and issues. Standard poodles are large dogs with all of the concerns that go along with active, bigger dogs. Whether clipped for a dog show or in a more utilitarian style, standard poodles are still big dogs and must be treated as such. Standard poodles are probably the most adaptable of the three poodle sizes.

Miniature poodles can often be devoted to one person. This penchant for being a "one person dog" is one of the reasons that minis often excel in obedience work. Miniature poodles should always be safeguarded from situations where their "bigger than I really am" attitude could get them into trouble.

While standard and miniature poodles are members of the American Kennel Club's Non-Sporting Breeds group, toy poodles are members of the AKC's Toy Group. The smallest poodles have become very popular pets, able competitors in the show ring, and no disgrace to their larger poodle-kin in winning obedience titles. Toy poodles, in the opinion of one breed expert, are somewhat like cats: "They can take you or leave you." Though toy poodles may be small, they still share much of the versatility and adaptability of standards and miniatures.

One of the great strengths of the poodle breed standard (the detailed, officially accepted, written description of the breed, see page 13) as developed by the Poodle Club of America (PCA) and sanctioned by the AKC is that, except for size, the standard for all three varieties is the same!

Both standard poodles and miniature poodles are much older varieties than the toy poodles of today. Much of the knowledge and skill that went into developing and improving the bigger

ter quality than the odd-looking assortment of so-called "toy poodles" of earlier years. Achieving small size without sacrificing the unique attributes of true poodles, a group of dedicated breeders literally recreated toy poodles in a smaller image of the stately standards and the popular miniatures.

Drawbacks to Poodles

Poodles in all three sizes will have their lives controlled in part by the breed's most visibly obvious, outward characteristic—their coat. In every situation tho curly poodle coat must be considered. An ungroomed poodle is very different from an ungroomed cocker spaniel, ungroomed schnauzer, or even an ungroomed beagle. Without regular attention, a poodle's curly coat can become unsightly, unpleasant to be around, and even unhealthy and unsafe.

Poodles also suffer some of the drawbacks that often come with being popular over a long span of time. There are more potential health problems involving poodles than plague many other breeds. Poodles must be purchased from a reputable, knowledgeable source to increase the odds of getting a quality, healthy pet. Because of poodles' intelligence, owners must become competent and consistent dog trainers. Poodles absolutely cannot be sometime pets relegated to the backyard; they must be allowed to share the life of their humans.

To sum up, it must be conceded that poodles are not the *perfect* dog for everyone, but with proper selection, grooming, care, attention, and training, poodles can come very close to being the best pets for many people. You can't put any dog on a shelf, to be brought out only for ornamentation and this is especially true of a breed that thrives on close and consistent human interaction.

From humble beginnings, the poodle rose to lofty heights, becoming the friend and confidant of presidents and kings. This apricot miniature puppy has its own regal demeanor.

sizes definitely helped to create and establish the modern toy poodles.

Even though poodles under 10 inches (25 cm) have been known for centuries, the toy poodles we have now are really a creation of recent decades. Prior to the 1920s, they were usually quite inferior to standards and miniatures in quality and consistency. American poodle breeders, working with some excellent miniatures, gradually produced toy poodles of much bet-

Advice for Potential Poodle Owners

1. Be absolutely certain that you want to own a poodle. Treat the purchase of a poodle as an investment, a labor-intensive, time-consuming investment that will only pay off in direct proportion to the amount of hard, smart work you put into it. The poodle coat alone will require a good deal of time and work to keep your potential pet looking and feeling good. Invest only in a healthy poodle from breeding stock known to be as free from inherited diseases and defects as possible, and that have test results to prove it. Avoid the "bargain" poodle like the plague!

2. Go where quality poodles are to be found. Visit as many dog shows as you can. Sit back and watch how the judge decides which poodle wins. Try to understand what makes one poodle better than another and try to gain the mental image of what a good poodle should look like.

3. Find yourself a poodle mentor, a respected breeder and/or exhibitor of poodles who will commit to be your teacher, confidant, and friend. Throughout this book, poodle mentors are mentioned as additional and invaluable sources of information, as on-hand problem solvers, and as guides through the sometimes perplexing maze of poodle ownership.

4. Find a local veterinarian to advise you about poodles, their potential health problems, and poodle ownership.

The American Kennel Club Standard for the Poodle

The standard for the poodle (toy variety) is the same for the standard and the miniature varieties except where height is concerned.

General Appearance, Carriage, and Condition—That of a very active, intelligent, and elegant-appearing dog, squarely built, well proportioned,

Some poodles' coats can be groomed into ringlet-like cords. Corded poodles were once popular enough to have their own breed club, but they are rarely seen now.

The expression on this stately, brown standard poodle's face clearly projects an image of the poodle as something stronger than a soft, pampered pet.

13

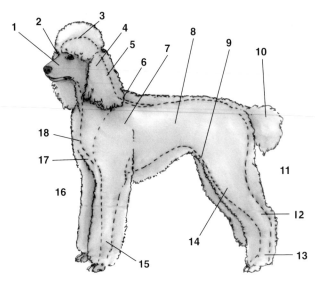

1. Skull, 2. Stop, 3. Skull, 4. Ear,
5. Neckline, 6. Withers, 7. Shoulder, 8. Rib
cage, 9. Loin, 10. Tail, 11. Hindquarters,
12. Hock, 13. Rear pastern, 14. Stifle
15. Front pastern, 16. Forequarters,
17. Brisket, 18. Chest

Value of Points

General appearance,
 temperament, carriage,
 and condition..............................30
Head, expression, ears,
 eyes, and teeth...........................20
Body, neck, legs, feet and tail 20
Gait...20
Coat, color and texture.................10

Disqualifications

Size—*A dog over or under the
height limits specified shall be disqualified.*

Clip—*A dog in any type of clip
other than those listed under Coat
shall be disqualified.*

Parti-colors—*The coat of a parti-
colored dog is not an even solid
color at the skin, but of two or more
colors. Parti-colored dogs shall be
disqualified.*

moving soundly and carrying himself
proudly. Properly clipped in the traditional fashion and carefully groomed,
the Poodle has about him an air of distinction and dignity peculiar to himself.

**Size, Proportion, Substance—
Size**—The **Standard Poodle** is over
15 inches (38 cm) at the highest point
of the shoulders. Any Poodle which is
15 inches (38 cm) or less in height
shall be *disqualified* from competition
as a Standard Poodle. **The Miniature
Poodle** is 15 inches (38 cm) or under
at the highest point of the shoulders,
with a minimum height in excess of 10
inches (25 cm). Any Poodle which is
over 15 inches (38 cm) or is 10 inches
(25 cm) or less at the highest point of
the shoulders shall be *disqualified*
from competition as a Miniature
Poodle. The **Toy Poodle** is 10 inches
(25 cm) or under at the highest point
of the shoulders. Any Poodle which is
more than 10 inches (25 cm) at the
highest point of the shoulders shall be
disqualified from competition as a Toy
Poodle. As long as the Toy Poodle is
definitely a Toy Poodle and the
Miniature Poodle a Miniature Poodle,
both in balance and proportion for the
Variety, diminutiveness shall be the
deciding factor when all other points
are equal. **Proportion:** To insure the
desirable squarely built appearance,
the length of body measured from the
breastbone to the point of the rump
approximates the height from the highest point of the shoulders to the
ground. **Substance:** Bone and muscle
of both forelegs and hind legs are in
proportion to the size of the dog.

Head and Expression: (a) Eyes—
very dark, oval in shape and set far
enough apart and positioned to create
an alert, intelligent expression. **Major
faults:** *Eyes round, protruding, large
or very light.* **(b) Ears** hanging close to
the head, set at or slightly below eye
level. The ear leather is long, wide,
and thickly feathered; however the ear

fringe should not be of excessive length. **(c)** *Skull* moderately rounded, with a slight but definite stop. Cheekbones and muscles flat. Length from occiput to stop about the same as length of muzzle. **(d)** *Muzzle* long, straight, and fine, with slight chiseling under the eyes. Strong without lippiness. The chin definite enough to preclude snipiness. *Major fault: Lack of chin.* **Teeth** white, strong, and with a scissors bite. *Major faults: Undershot, overshot, wry mouth.*

Neck, Topline, Body—Neck well proportioned, strong, and long enough to permit the head to be carried high and with dignity. Skin snug at throat. The neck rises from strong, smoothly muscled shoulders. *Major fault:* Ewe neck. The *topline* is level, neither sloping nor roached, from the highest point of the shoulder blade to the base of the tail, with the exception of a slight hollow just behind the shoulder. **Body (a)** Chest deep and moderately wide with well sprung ribs. **(b)** The loin is short, broad, and muscular. **(c)** Tail straight, set on high and carried up, docked of sufficient length to insure a balanced outline. *Major fault: Set low, curled, carried over the back.*

Forequarters—Strong, smoothly muscled shoulders. The shoulder blade is well laid back and approximately the same length as the upper foreleg. *Major fault: Steep shoulder.* **(a)** *Forelegs* straight and parallel when viewed from the front. When viewed from the side, the elbow is directly below the highest point of the shoulder. The pasterns are strong. Dewclaws may be removed.

Feet—The feet are rather small, oval in shape with toes well arched and cushioned on thick, firm pads. Nails short but not excessively shortened. The feet turn neither in nor out. *Major faults: Paper or splay foot.*

Hindquarters—The angulation of the hindquarters balances that of the

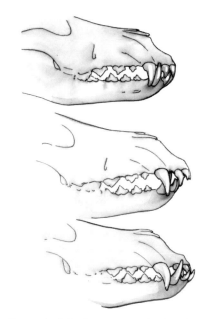

How a dog's teeth come together is called its bite; Top—scissors bite, Center—overbite, Bottom—underbite.

forequarters. **(a)** *Hind legs* straight and parallel when viewed from the rear. Muscular with width in the region of the stifles which are well bent; femur and tibia are about equal in length; hock to heel short and perpendicular to the ground. When standing, the rear toes are only slightly behind the point of the rump. *Major fault: Cow-hocks.*

Coat—(a) *Quality* **(1)** Curly: Of naturally harsh texture, dense throughout. **(2)** Corded: Hanging in tight, even cords of varying length; longer on the mane and body coat, head and ears; shorter on puffs, bracelets, and pompons. **(b) Clip**—A poodle under 12 months may be shown in the "Puppy" clip. In all regular classes, poodles 12 months or older must be shown in the "English Saddle" or "Continental" clip. In the Stud Dog or Brood Bitch classes, and in a non-competitive

Parade of Champions, Poodles may be shown in the "Sporting" clip. A Poodle shown in any other type of clip shall be *disqualified*.

(1) *Puppy*: A Poodle under a year old may be shown in the "Puppy" clip with the coat long. The face, throat, feet, and base of tail are shaved. The entire shaven foot is visible. There is a pompon on the end of the tail. In order to give a neat appearance and a smooth unbroken line, shaping of the coat is permissible. **(2) *"English Saddle":*** In the "English Saddle" clip, the face, throat, feet, forelegs, and base of tail are shaved, leaving puffs on the forelegs and a pompon on the end of the tail. The hindquarters are covered with a short blanket of hair except for a curved shaved area on each flank and two shaved bands on each hind leg. The entire shaven foot and a portion of the shaven leg above the puff are visible. The rest of the body is left in full coat but may be shaped in order to insure overall balance. **(3) *"Continental":*** In the "Continental" clip, the face, throat, feet, and base of tail are shaved. The hindquarters are shaved with pompons (optional) on the hips. The legs are shaved, leaving bracelets on the hind legs and puffs on the forelegs. There is a pompon on the end of the tail. The entire shaven foot and a portion of the shaven foreleg above the puff are visible. The rest of the body is left in full coat, but may be shaped to insure overall balance. **(4) *"Sporting":*** In the "Sporting" clip, a Poodle shall be shown with face, feet, throat, and base of tail shaved, leaving a scissored cap on the top of the head and a pompon on the end of the tail. The rest of the body and legs are clipped or scissored to follow the outline of the dog, leaving a short blanket of coat no longer than one inch (2.45 cm) in length. The hair on the legs may be slightly longer than that on the body.

In all clips, the hair of the topknot may be left free or held in place by elastic bands. The hair is only of sufficient length to present a smooth outline. "Topknot" refers only to hair on the skull, from stop to occiput. This is the only area where elastic bands may be used.

Color—The coat is an even and solid color at the skin. In blues, grays, silvers, browns, cafe-au-laits, apricots, and creams the coat may show varying shades of the same color. This is frequently present in somewhat darker feathering of the ears and in the tipping of the ruff. While clear colors are definitely preferred, such natural variation in the shading of the coat is not to be considered a fault. Brown and cafe-au-lait Poodles have liver-colored noses, eye rims and lips, dark toenails and dark amber eyes. Black, blue, gray, silver, cream, and white poodles have black noses, eye rims and lips, black or self-colored toenails, and very dark eyes. In the apricots, while the foregoing coloring is preferred, liver-colored noses, eye rims and lips, and amber eyes are permitted but are not desirable. *Major faults: Color of nose, lips, and eye rims incomplete or of wrong color for color of dog.*

Parti-colored dogs shall be *disqualified*. The coat of a parti-colored dog is not an even, solid color at the skin, but is of two or more colors.

Gait—A straightforward trot with light springy action and strong hindquarters drive. Head and tail carried up. Sound, effortless movement is essential.

Temperament—Carrying himself proudly, very active, intelligent, the Poodle has about him an air of distinction and dignity peculiar to himself. *Major faults: Shyness or sharpness.*

Major Faults—Any distinct deviation from the desired characteristics described in the Breed Standard.

Understanding Poodles

Characteristic Poodle Behavior

Poodles have become the breed they are because of their closeness to humans for so many hundreds of years. Retrievers, courtiers, circus performers, or just pets, poodles made their way with their intelligence, personality, and companionability. Poodles in any of the three sizes usually become devoted companions. Many poodle breeders avow that their dogs seem able to anticipate human needs, wishes, and expectations.

Most dogs need to be fed, watered, and walked at the same time every day. Adaptable though they are, poodles may need routine in their lives a little more than some other breeds do. A person whose life is based on a muddled, disorganized, or "catch-as-catch-can" format is probably not the best owner for a poodle. Poodles need consistency in their lives. While they are not canine automatons, they do like to get into a regular pattern.

Though usually quite friendly, poodles can also sometimes be aloof with strangers. There are countless poodle stories about a dog that absolutely ignored someone until it was clear to it that this person was worthy of acceptance.

Perhaps the key behavioral characteristic of poodles is the breed's innate desire to please its owner. This gives poodle owners an added responsibility in helping the dog know just what is expected of it. Unless the human is clear about what behavior is satisfactory and what is not, how can the dog know?

Poodles need a lot of affection, attention, and care. Problems with poodles occur when any of these three ingredients is missing. A poodle cannot know that an owner didn't give it a pat because he or she had a bad day at the office. The dog only knows it didn't get the customary sign of affection. A poodle that can't get your attention in a positive way is much like a child in discovering a less than positive way to catch your eye. It is also true that,

This white standard poodle shows off the sculptured look of the popular continental clip. Duck hunters began clipping their poodles to protect their retriever's internal organs from frigid water while freeing up its hindquarters as an aid in swimming. Compare this poodle with the corded poodle on page 13.

17

Poodles have been excellent companion dogs for centuries. It is a role that they cherish.

while poodles are tougher than their detractors will admit, they do need quality care to be quality pets.

Poodles also have what could be described as a definite sense of

humor. They do funny things and appreciate the responses they get for their actions. Poodles seem to know when they have an appreciative audience and ham it up just for few more laughs or smiles. If you fail to understand the poodle sense of humor, you fail to truly understand the poodle.

Poodles as Pets

There can be no better pet than a dog from a breed that has been chosen for its pet qualities for several hundred years. Poodles have a heritage in which their companion qualities transformed them from sporting dogs to pets. When a poodle comes from a good genetic background, receives good care, and is well trained, a quality pet is usually the final result.

Poodles as Show Dogs

If the dog show hadn't been in existence when the poodle came along, someone would have had to invent it. Poodles, perhaps even to their detriment, have become among the showiest of dog breeds. Watching a perfectly groomed poodle move smoothly around a show ring is the picture in many people's minds when dog shows are mentioned.

Poodles seem to know when they are on display. Many poodle fans tell of occasions when a poodle of moderate quality goes into the show ring and an amazing transformation seems to occur. The formerly quiet and reserved dog sometimes walks away with the prize by really strutting its stuff, by catching the judge's eye, and by keeping it.

Poodles in Obedience Work

Poodles excel in the show ring in part because of the combined arts of dog breeding and dog grooming. They do well in obedience due to a combination of the skills of dog breeding and dog training. Poodles add much dash

Dog shows and poodles seem to be made for each other! Poodles win as many show championships as any other breed and more than most.

and charm to their show ring competing, but it is in obedience that the blending of two innate poodle characteristics really shines: their exceptional intelligence and their deep, abiding desire to please their owner. When you have a bright dog you are blessed. When you have a bright, *motivated* dog you are twice blessed!

Poodles have done exceedingly well in obedience trials since obedience trials began, both in Europe and the United States. Obedience trials, such as those sanctioned by the American Kennel Club, allow dogs and owners to pursue a number of obedience titles. Among them are Companion Dog (CD), Companion Dog Excellent (CDX), Utility Dog (UD), and Utility Dog Excellent (UDX). Each of these obedience titles, and several other advanced and specialized degrees, is an acknowledgment that both dog and trainer have worked hard on an increasingly difficult set of commands performed under varying conditions.

When a show dog wins enough points in conformation competition (against other dogs) it becomes a champion, a title that comes *before* the dog's name, as in Champion Amanda's Sportboy. A noncompetitive obedience title is added *after* the name, such as Silver Bloom of Home, CDX. (Several competitive obedience titles do go before the dog's name, such as the Obedience Trial Champion [OTCH] and others). Dog fanciers are fond of pointing out that a truly exceptional dog has a title both at the beginning and the ending of its name, as Champion Editor's Revenge, UD. Titles fore and aft convey a great deal of information about the quality of a poodle both as a handsome show dog and as a well-trained obedience dog.

Part of poodle ownership means at least considering obedience training and trials if a poodle shows any promise in that direction. Obedience trials are usually held in conjunction with

Poodles are among the top performers in obedience and agility trials.

dog shows. Skilled obedience judges conduct the trials and grade each dog on its performance in following its owner's commands. Obedience work isn't easy, but most poodle owners involved in obedience consider it very rewarding and well worth the effort!

Poodles as Retrievers

Modern poodles certainly pose no threat to replace Labrador retrievers as the most popular breed used in hunting and in retriever trials, but some poodles do still serve in their ancient role and continue to do it well.

Even in the modern retriever breeds, some dogs simply don't do as well as others. Generally, if you want a working retriever, of any breed, seek a dog that has a number of actual retrievers in its close family background. If your desire is to own a poodle that can work as a retriever, contact the Poodle Club of America (see Useful Addresses and Literature, page 101), which may be able to put you in touch with a poodle breeder who specializes

Poodles went from duck hunting to circuses and carnivals. This black miniature shows a flair for entertainment that makes you almost ignore the beautiful flowers in the background.

in breeding poodles for retrieving. Occasionally, someone will uncover retrieving aptitude in a poodle from an exhibition and/or obedience background. These dogs need just a little

This silver miniature shows off its puppy clip, a clip that show dogs can wear until they are one year old.

encouragement and training to become quite adequate in the role that was once the primary duty of poodles.

Other Poodle Contributions

Poodle fans are generally an adventurous lot. They have been willing to demonstrate the versatility of their breed in as many venues as possible. Poodle teams have pulled dogsleds in dog races in competition with the northern breeds, such as Malamutes and huskies. Poodles have been taught to herd livestock. They have served as war dogs and have gone along with trailing hounds in search of game. Poodles have been guide dogs for the sight-impaired and therapy dogs. John Steinbeck's Charley traveled all across the United States with his Pulitzer Prize-winning author/owner.

Poodle Mixes

Some dog breeders have crossed the poodle with other kinds of dogs. Most people have heard of these dogs of mixed-poodle ancestry, but may not recognize them for what they are—mixed-breed or mongrel dogs! These crossbreds are often given clever designations such as, "cock-a-poos," "peke-a-poos," and so forth, and have been widely sold as pets. They may sometimes be good pets but they are not, in *any* way purebred and as such, each "something-a-poo" should certainly be spayed or neutered! There have also been crosses between standard poodles and wolves and other wild canines to study coat inheritance and other genetic matters. One of the most interesting crosses involves the British blending of the poodle with the Labrador retriever. This cross, referred to as the "Labradoodle" was made to put the poodle's curly, non-shed coat on a stockier body to serve as a guide dog for the blind. Early reports state that the poodle-Lab mixture has performed well as a guide dog.

Sharing Your Home with a Poodle

Choosing to bring a poodle into your life may require you to make some lifestyle modifications:

• You may not be able to take spur-of-the-moment trips because you must consider your dog.

• Entertaining guests in your home may mean arranging for the safety and comfort of your dog.

• Housekeeping chores that you might have neglected for yourself must be done to avoid compounding the work when a curious poodle gets into a half-eaten pizza left on the coffee table.

Adding a poodle to your life is more than just getting a dog to keep in the backyard. Poodles are companion pets. They need closeness with their humans to complete and to comple-ment their lives.

Poodles' Coats

Whether your poodle is a tiny toy, an active miniature, or a large standard, one factor is a constant—the coat. The poodle coat, the breed's trademark, should be the same for all three sizes. It is dense and curly and will require regular brushing and regular grooming to look its best (see Grooming, page 67). Brushing will be your job and can take a couple of hours per week or more. Grooming is often best left up to professional dog groomers whose expertise in trimming, shaping, and washing is well worth whatever it costs.

The poodle's coat does have a strong positive—it does not shed like the coats of other canines. This one element accounts for much of the popularity of the poodle with people who have allergies. The poodle's coat may require a lot of care, but it doesn't contribute to airborne particles like the hair of most other dog breeds.

Your poodle will not be content exiled to a kennel or to a backyard. A neglected poodle can be one sorry-looking specimen! Owning a poodle

Athletic ability and intelligence are in evidence as this black miniature completes a jump on her way, successfully, to a coveted obedience title.

Children and poodles make a happy combination, but young children should always be supervised to protect the poodle from unintentional injury.

their high degree of intelligence. Show poodles not only must win by looking good; they must be amenable to training. Pet poodles are perhaps the smartest poodles of them all. Pet dogs make their way *not* on their ability to retrieve, perform in an obedience trial, or win in a show ring. Pet poodles must adapt to their owners' wishes, moods, and needs and try to fill these in the best poodle-like fashion.

Owning a poodle is different from owning a mixed breed or a dog of some other breed. If you are to have a successful relationship with a smart poodle, you must be a smart poodle owner! You need to recognize that inconsistencies negatively affect smarter dogs more. To act one way one time and another way another time may confuse a poodle and make it distrustful of you.

Poodles and Children

Poodles and children can have happy lifelong relationships. Poodles are affectionate and devoted to their young masters and mistresses. Some children, on the other hand, are sometimes neglectful and even cruel to animals. Cruel, unfair treatment could turn a loving, trusting poodle into a distrusting and fearful pet.

Children should always be supervised when playing with a pet. Wise owners will take time to teach children the proper, caring, and acceptable way to treat a dog. When children recognize that poodles are more than just movable, plush, stuffed animals, they are more apt to gain a real understanding of how to act correctly around a pet.

Poodles and the Elderly

Poodles are excellent pets for people who have reached seniorhood. Poodles are loving, devoted, and willing companion animals. Many stories abound in poodle lore about older peo-

means seeing that the dog doesn't become a tangled, matted, unsightly jumble of curly dog hair. If you want to own a poodle, its coat must always be a consideration.

Smart Dogs Need Smart Owners

One of the main reasons that poodles aren't the right dog for every individual or every family centers on the basic intelligence of the breed. Poodles have lived in close quarters with human beings for hundreds of years. Because humans tend not to suffer with stupid dogs under these circumstances, a type of intense selection for intelligence took place.

When poodles were retrievers they needed intelligence. When they got into "show biz" with the early traveling carnivals and circuses, smart dogs were again necessary. Poodles that have surpassed many other breeds in obedience trials amply demonstrate

ple who had never had a dog before and who became inseparable with their first poodle. Lonely people can find great solace in the tender attentions of a well-behaved poodle. Retirees whose lives sometime lack the structure of their working years can find routine and order in the schedule that must be followed in caring for a poodle. Brushing can keep older arms and hands supple, and walks with the poodle are good exercise for dog and human alike.

Poodles and older people have a lot to offer each other. Poodles need loving owners who will see that the dogs' needs are met. In addition to companionship and a reason for the elderly person to get out of the house, poodles offer some protection from intruders by serving as early-warning systems. Poodles, because of their barking presence, have been praised by law enforcement officials for being absolute deterrents to burglars and other criminals.

Poodles and Other Pets

Poodles usually adapt well with other pet animals in a home setting. While it is important to show all pets the necessary attention to stave off petty jealousies, poodles aren't usually troublemakers.

For the owner who takes the time, as gradually as possible, to introduce a new poodle puppy into a household where cats live, the results can be very gratifying. Cats and poodles can learn to peacefully coexist, and once they do, they often become close pals. Human supervision to oversee the early interactions between pets can avoid most problems. Feeding two pets separately, at least for a while, is recommended. Leaving a young poodle alone with an existing pet is certainly unwise until the two have accepted each other.

Poodles and other dogs are usually no problem. Not usually aggressive, poodles can hold their own in the "pecking order" that household pets often establish. Supervise first contacts between the existing pets and the new to avoid any initial problems. After a pet already in place comes to understand that the poodle isn't a threat and has its own place in the family, most trouble ceases.

Keep the Poodle a *Real* Dog

Poodles have a long and distinguished history of being *real* dogs in service to *real* people. Just because some people treat their poodle like a canine Barbie doll doesn't negate the fact that the poodle is a living creature with all that brings, good and bad. Buy a poodle to be an actual dog and not as a plaything. The poodle will suffer greatly if viewed as an object and you will suffer by never getting to know all the joys that being a poodle owner can bring.

This young apricot standard shows the poodle's naturally happy disposition.

Caring for Your Poodle

Housing a Poodle

Some breeds actually thrive on being both inside and outside dogs. This is not the case with poodles. That is not to say that poodles don't enjoy being outside—they do. Poodles are, however, more human-oriented than some breeds. Where herd guardian breeds like Great Pyrenees or Anatolian sheepdogs are often uncomfortable away from their flocks, poodles show much the same discomfort when away from their human family.

It is possible for a poodle to adjust to living in a doghouse in a suburban backyard, but that would be a sad fate for any poodle. Poodles crave the companionship of human beings, especially their own human beings. To attempt to make a poodle into only an occasional pet is to engage in one of the cruelest forms of animal abuse. Don't buy a poodle if you don't want it to be near you!

To many dogs, especially strays and homeless dogs, a suburban backyard with a warm doghouse and plenty of food and fresh water would seem like canine heaven. Not so with the poodle! The suburban backyard without the poodle's human family would be like solitary confinement in a dismal prison. Again, don't buy a poodle if you want to have the dog near you only when it is convenient. A poodle will not understand why you will want it near at times and away at other times. Spare the dog this confusion, this frustration, and this sadness.

Housing for a poodle should be *with* you in your home. A cage/crate/carrier will provide all that your dog will need for those times when it must be absent from you. Inside, with you, is the best place for a dog that adores you. For those brief and temporary times when your poodle may need to be out of your home, a draft-free dog house in a fenced backyard or kennel run is useful, but only when *absolutely* necessary.

The Poodle and Exercise

Exercise is an important element in any poodle's life. While a poodle is quite content to stay by the side of your easy chair, long walks with you, jogs in the park, or hiking in the country will also be enjoyable, but only if you are along. If you want your poodle to get enough exercise, you'll have to go along. One dog expert stated, "There are dogs that will pull you along on a walk and dogs that will ignore you entirely, but the poodle goes for the walk only because you are going for a walk too!"

Standard poodles are robust, strong, large dogs. While they aren't usually as hyperactive as some breeds, they do enjoy running. They need consistency in their exercise to remain in good condition. Consistency will mean some exercise *every day*, not some exercise every week or so! Some poodle owners who don't enjoy actually running alongside their poodles will get long leashes, especially those on a handheld reel. These owners will keep their dogs on leash and will let the dogs circle them at whatever pace and at whatever distance (up to the end of the leash) the dog chooses.

HOW-TO:
Traveling by Air with Your Poodle

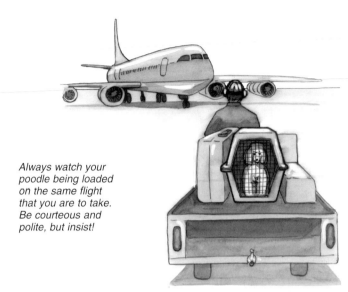

Going places with your poodle will involve planning and preparation. The main issue on every trip with a pet should be maximizing the dog's safety and comfort. Because of their usually in-home lifestyles, most poodles should be crate-trained. This greatly simplifies traveling as the poodle's bedroom/den actually goes with the dog. Crates also add to the safety of a dog while a vehicle, train, or plane is in motion.

Unless you are absolutely certain that you can purchase the same brand of dog food at your destination that your poodle eats at home, be sure to include enough food in your luggage for the entire trip.

There have been many improvements in air travel for pets in recent decades. A poodle in an airline-approved carrier is welcomed on most of the larger overseas and domestic airlines.

Always watch your poodle being loaded on the same flight that you are to take. Be courteous and polite, but insist!

When traveling with your poodle, make every effort to keep it safe and comfortable.

(If your poodle has something other than an approved carrier for its den/sleeping area, such carriers are usually available on a rental basis from the airlines. Call ahead to be certain.)

To enhance the ease and safety of your poodle's traveling, there are some good "rules of the road" to follow:

• Long before you plan to travel by air—even before you make your flight reservations—contact the airline you plan to use for their most current regulations about traveling with a pet. Ask the airline for any hints or suggestions about how to insure the safety and comfort of your poodle. Some smaller poodles may even be allowed as carry-on luggage, which lets the dog ride, in its carrier, in the passenger section with you.

• Consult your veterinarian about any reasons that your poodle should stay at home. Very young poodles, older dogs, and pets in poor health should probably not make a long and potentially stressful trip. The veterinarian can also provide you with a health certificate, which most airlines require for pet passengers. This certificate must be dated no more than ten days before the date of your flight. You also could ask your veterinarian about the advisability of motion-sickness or tranquilizer prescriptions for your traveling poodle.

• Your airline reservations should be made well in advance, making certain that the reservation clerk knows that you and your poodle will travel together. If the dog can't ride as carry-on luggage and must be placed in the cargo/baggage compartment, book a direct flight—if possible—to your destination, which will not necessitate changing planes. Even if you have to drive to a hub airport, a direct flight is always preferable.

• If your poodle has to ride in the baggage area, be certain to actually observe your pet being loaded on the plane, before you board it yourself. This is another reason that you should arrive very early for your flight.

• If you are traveling to another country, be certain that you meet all the entry requirements for bringing a dog into that country. Also be sure of the re-entry requirements you will have to face when leaving your destination and returning home.

• Double-check the airline carrier (your own or a rental) to make sure that the bolts holding it together are all tightened down and that the door and latch work correctly. Also make certain that the "conversion kit" for a water dish is attached so it can be filled from outside the carrier, if necessary.

• Prominently affix "Live Animal" stickers to the outside of the carrier. Be certain that you have attached a luggage tag with your name, address, and home phone number along with your destination and a phone number there.

• Include in the carrier a freshly laundered pad or blanket for the added comfort of your poodle. Be sure to put in one of your poodle's favorite toys to help lessen loneliness and boredom.

When traveling in an automobile, a pet should always ride in its carrier to avoid injuries that could come from being tossed around the car in the event of sudden stops, sharp turns, or accidents.

• Do not feed your pet for eight to ten hours prior to your flight's departure. You can water and exercise your poodle up to two hours before flight time. In order to prevent your pet and its carrier from becoming a soggy mess, do not put any food or water (other than in the external conversion kit waterer) in the carrier.

• While airline personnel are generally quite service-oriented, you should always assume a firm, but courteous, attitude with them. Clearly assure them that you greatly value your pet and expect every standard of pet comfort and safety to be met.

• One breeder suggests taking a picture of your poodle with you for identification purposes. Another puts a small lock on the carrier door (with an extra key taped to the top of the carrier under duct tape). Still another dog owner always photographs her pet as it is being loaded onto the plane.

• Be certain to get the names and employee numbers of as many as possible of the key people handling the transportation of your pet. (If things don't go well, you know who to blame; if things go well you know who to thank.)

Appealing charm is written all over this silver toy peeking from its pillow. Every poodle should have its own special home-within-the home.

Not all poodle trims are as ornate as the continental and the English saddle. This poodle is comfortable in its easy-to-keep sporting clip.

Traveling by Automobile

A poodle's nearness to its human family will often involve the dog in many short car trips. Longer trips do require planning and preparation, not unlike air travel with a dog, but don't become careless just because your poodle is often a passenger in your automobile.

As fine a companion pet as your poodle may be, it is still just a dog. You can't expect any dog to understand, avoid, and overcome all the physical hazards that can befall a pet in unknown territory. If you allow your poodle to stray away, even for just one moment, that could be the last time you will see your poodle alive! Be cautious about seeing that your poodle is kept with you and safe. Whether you and your poodle are taking a trip across town or across the country, there are some good, common sense rules to follow:

• Always let your poodle ride in its carrier whenever it goes with you in an automobile. A second choice would be to fasten the poodle into a canine safety belt or harness available in pet supply stores. Never let your pet ride unrestrained in a vehicle.

• Follow the same feeding and watering suggestions made about air travel (see HOW-TO: Traveling by Air with Your Poodle, page 26) when you and your poodle embark on long auto trips.

• If your trip lasts several hours or more, stop every hour or so to allow your pet to have some on-leash and well-supervised exercise and a relief break. A brief drink of water is permissible, but skip food and treats until you stop for the day.

• Never leave your poodle in a parked car unless you leave the motor running and the air conditioner on! Any day when temperatures reach as high as 60°F (16°C) can turn your parked family car, even with the windows partially down, into an automotive version of a solar oven (see Heatstroke, page 87)

• Always carefully plan and prepare for any overnight trips. Check with auto clubs, travel guides, and the long-distance reservation numbers of hotel/motel chains to be certain that your well-behaved poodle will be a welcomed guest in your room. Never try to slip a pet into a lodging place that you know doesn't allow pets. That is against the law and also further prejudices innkeepers against allowing pet guests.

Leaving Your Poodle Home

There are trips that may not lend themselves to your poodle going with you and there are circumstances that make a long trip with your dog impossible.

Boarding

If you can't take your poodle with you, one of your options is to board your dog. While being away from your poodle may be somewhat traumatic for both of you, boarding can be a very good alternative.

Boarding kennels have become much more numerous and much more professionally managed than they were some decades ago. Most boarding kennel owners and managers are dog people themselves and take excellent care of their lodgers. The American Boarding Kennel Association has a list of accredited kennels in your area. Write or phone the ABKA for further information (see Useful Addresses and Literature, page 101).

Many veterinarians handle boarding for their regular patients (which is what your poodle should be). Since your poodle is already known at the veterinary clinic, your absence may be less stressful.

Another option for boarding your poodle might be the breeder from whom you purchased the dog. Many times breeders don't mind taking in an old friend that is well mannered and healthy. Also, you should certainly

This white standard puppy sitting demurely next to some red tulips invites a comparison of which is more attractive.

have some experienced poodle breeders as friends and mentors who may help you out and put your pup up for a few days.

You may be able to leave your pet in your home while you travel if you have a trusted relative, friend, or neighbor who can provide in-home care. This is a very good option for many dogs.

Pet Sitters

In a similar manner, pet sitters are now available in most parts of the country. These licensed and bonded individuals are able to handle your dog's care in a caring and skillful manner. Ask your veterinarian or at a pet supply shop for the names of pet sitters in your area. Always ask for references and then check out these references before you leave on your trip.

Less than Obvious Needs

Caring for your poodle clearly means providing the dog with a good home, good food, good training, and a safe environment. Poodles do need more than these obvious needs to flourish; they need your affection, your attention, and your good judgment to make their lives better.

Love

Loving your poodle may seem like a easy need to fill, yet some people with poodles fail at it miserably. It is not enough to love an adorable poodle puppy. You must love the dog when it is an awkward adolescent, and even more so when it is an aging senior. You must love the dog when it does things that make you proud, and love it when it does things that embarrass you or cost you money.

Attention

Like other members of your household, your poodle will need its share of your time every day. Giving your pooch a cursory pat on the head when you come in tired from your job may not seem like much to you. To your poodle, your attention, and the touch of your hand is an absolutely thrilling reward. A kind word and a little playtime are prizes of great worth for your poodle.

If you are too busy to give your poodle the daily attention it needs to thrive, then you are too busy to own a poodle or any other dog. Factor the time you need to spend with your pet into your schedule. If you can't give this caring dog at least an hour a day, then wait until you can before you buy a poodle.

Good Judgment

Your poodle will depend on you for the decisions that affect its life. Use good judgment when deciding these issues:
• Don't give your poodle table scraps that could lead to obesity and other health problems.
• Don't let your poodle ride unrestrained in your car.
• Don't let small children, or unruly older children, hurt your poodle through rough and careless play. Always supervise them.
• Teach children the right way to treat animals.
• Don't let poodles go without regular grooming.
• Always visit the veterinarian with your dog at least two times each year.
• Remember that your poodle is an investment and protect this investment in every way possible!

Before You Buy a Poodle

Poodles are beautiful. Poodles are stylish. Poodles are smart. Poodles attract attention. None of these reasons is the *right* reason to own a poodle. There are people who want to be seen walking down the street with a perfectly groomed poodle. The use of a canine just as a status symbol is certainly not a right reason to own any dog.

The *right* reason to own a poodle is to have a canine companion that will share your life. The poodle is well equipped to be just the answer for someone who wants a dog as a friend. If one wants a sometime plaything, let them choose a stuffed animal and leave the poodles (and all other dogs as well) alone.

Making the Right Decision

Some points that you should factor into your decision to own a poodle are:

1. Is each person in your home really aware of what owning a poodle will entail?

2. Has each person agreed to help care for this poodle and help it develop as it should and keep it safe and comfortable?

3. Will each family member take time every day to show affection and attention to the poodle?

4. Is your family ready to make the financial investment that a quality poodle puppy will require (perhaps several hundred dollars in initial cost), including all the food, grooming ($20 to $35 each time if done by a professional groomer), and veterinary care it may need?

5. Is there one specific, responsible person in your family who can spend several days at home to help a bewildered poodle puppy settle in?

These questions should not be casually answered. If your family can't faithfully do these things, you should wait before purchasing a poodle. Save yourself some heartache and an innocent poodle puppy a false start in life by being mature enough, and unselfish enough, to put off what may not be a good idea right now.

Toy, Miniature, or Standard?

Few breeds can give you the size options you have with the poodle. The breed standard stresses that the three poodle varieties should be identical

Teacup poodles are very tiny toy poodles, so tiny that they may not be able to reproduce and can have numerous health problems.

Poodles are far tougher than many people realize. A team of standard poodles have even competed successfully in grueling sled dog races, like Alaska's famous Iditarod.

These three unclipped house pet poodles, two standards (black and white) and one miniature (brown) provide quite a contrast to those dogs with one of the accepted poodle clips.

except for size (see pages 00–00). The size decision is one that can be based purely on your own preferences. You should know that height and not weight is the deciding factor as to whether a poodle is a standard, miniature, or toy. It is possible that a chunky toy poodle could actually weigh more than a thin miniature. Weight is not even mentioned in the AKC poodle standard.

Toys: Toy poodles, under 10 inches (25 cm) in height at the shoulder, have gained greatly in popularity. While they are obviously smaller than standards and miniature, they are still all poodle. Bear in mind, however, that toys aren't always the best choice when very small children are in the home. These little poodles are sometimes quite vocal, but they share the same love and devotion for their owners that all poodles possess.

There are very tiny toy poodles called "teacup poodles." Teacups have been produced by breeding together increasingly smaller and smaller dogs. One respected poodle breeder sheds light on these tiny dogs by stating that teacups affect their owners in two ways: (1) in the pocketbook, from all the added health expenses; and (2) in the heart, from having to watch the teacup poodle suffer from abnormalities and inherited illnesses until it finally dies a very early death.

Miniatures: Miniature poodles, the most popular of the poodles, fit that special niche for those who want a dog that is between a small toy poodle and the strapping standard poodle. Many miniatures share the best aspects of both the other sizes and have these qualities in a tidy, but not tiny, package. Miniatures are over 10 inches (25 cm) in height, but less than 15 (37.5 cm) tall measured at the dog's shoulder. Regardless of what a poodle's papers may say, if it is over this height limit the dog is a standard.

If a poodle is under the 10-inch (25 cm) height limit, it is a toy.

Standards: Standard poodles are over 15 inches (37.5 cm) and often quite a few inches over. Standards are good pets for people who prefer a larger dog. Like miniatures and toys, standards retain all the best poodle characteristics. These largest poodles still have the playfulness of their smaller counterparts, but blend it with a certain dignity.

Standard poodles require more room and exercise than their smaller kin. Both miniatures and toys have surged ahead of the bigger poodles in popularity. This may stem from the added requirements that larger dogs bring to a modern dog owner. Higher fences, stronger gates, more items to put out of Pierre's way are all additional purchases for those who prefer a standard. These big poodles can be effective deterrents to unwanted visitors and they also often show a seriousness of demeanor that makes even some youngsters seem wise beyond their years.

A Puppy or an Older Poodle?

The devotion that most poodles show for their previous owners could be a negative against an adult. It is difficult for some dogs, even some poodles, to adjust to a new master or mistress. Judge any adult poodles that may be offered to you strictly on an individual basis. Unless there is a valid reason for this adult poodle to be available, such as a relocation where the dog could not go along, a divorce where no one gets the dog, or a death in a family, you might be obtaining a dog with medical or behavioral problems. A puppy can be what you mold it to be but you won't actually know if an adult can fit with you or you with it.

On the plus side for obtaining an adult is the fact that it will still need your love, care, and attention, but cer-

This exercise is designed to judge a dog's agility. This white miniature completes the jump easily and then tops it off by having a good time while doing it!

tainly not the initial amount of time that a puppy will require. If you want a poodle, but you don't have time to devote to a puppy, and an adult is available with a logical reason for it being on the market, try the older dog. Many poodle fans began in just this fashion several poodles ago.

A respected veteran poodle breeder (who knows you and trusts you to provide a dog a good home), the PCA, or the PCA poodle rescue organization (see Useful Addresses and Literature, page 101) may know of adult poodles that need good homes. If you think an adult poodle might fit into your lifestyle, don't hesitate to look into the possibilities. There may be an adult

Choosing a poodle puppy is always an enjoyable experience. Doing everything to help that puppy grow into a well-behaved adult isn't always fun, but it certainly is worth it!

that is just what you need, but take this approach only on the basis of sound advice.

Male or Female?

Poodles of either sex can make excellent pets. Both males and females can do well in the hot competition of the show ring. Both male and female poodles have excelled in obedience work. The choice of the sex of your potential poodle is largely one of personal preference. Male poodles, even toys, are generally "all male," but without the excessive "macho" behavior of some breeds. Female poodles are, by definition, quite feminine, perhaps a bit more refined in appearance, and often a little smaller.

Unspayed female poodles go into a three-week-long heat cycle about twice a year. The inconvenience of having to protect an unspayed female from amorous male dogs and the added bother of in-season discharge for a dog

that stays indoors make owning an unspayed female a bit more challenging. Spaying a non-breeding female solves both of these problems and a number of other health concerns as well (see False Pregnancy, page 95).

Males have a tendency to mark their territory with urine. This isn't a problem outside in the backyard or at the relief spot, but an unhousebroken male (and some housebroken males) poodle may carry this marking behavior inside with him. Unneutered males are also preoccupied with females that are in heat. You will have to be extra careful about your poodle escaping from your supervision when a nearby female is in season.

While spayed or neutered dogs cannot be shown in American Kennel Club conformation shows, they can show their skills in obedience trials. Spaying or neutering is one of the very best things you can do for your poodle. Unless you are in that tiny fraction of a percentage of people who have a poodle that really is worth keeping intact as breeding stock, your poodle should certainly be neutered or spayed. Such operations on males or females will not decrease their pet qualities and will eliminate the chances of unplanned puppies that will only add to the glut of pups that already fill animal shelters to overflowing.

What Color?

Poodles come in some of the most beautiful solid colors in all of dogdom. The blacks, whites, blues, browns, apricots, grays, creams, cafe-au-laits, silvers, and other accepted poodle colors all have their advocates. Blacks and whites are more popular for dog shows, but browns, grays, and even the apricots are often seen in the show ring. Rarer colors are usually more expensive, but no top-quality poodle of any color is cheap. Unless you absolutely must have a specific color, search for the best poodle puppy available regardless of color. Choose quality of the total dog over a lesser dog of just the right color.

Be leery of buying a poodle that has tan markings on its face and legs. Such poodles have what is called "phantom" coloring where tan markings appear. Other poodles may come in white with spots of other colors. While both of these may be attractive, such markings are disqualifications in American dog shows and could be a sign of impure breeding.

Prospective poodle buyers should know that some of the dilute colors—grays, blues, or silvers—may be born black. These poodle pups will usually get increasingly lighter as they mature.

Color is a personal preference. If you absolutely have your heart set on an apricot poodle, seek out the best apricot you can find and that you can afford. Color is another area of poodle ownership that requires study to gain understanding. If your goal is the best possible pet, and size, sex, and color aren't that important, the poodle is the breed for you!

Show Quality or Pet Quality?

Show dogs of all breeds and especially of a popular and widely exhibited breed like the poodle are the products of generation after generation of carefully planned breedings. Thousands of poodle breeders have diligently studied, worked, restudied, and reworked to produce the very best poodles that have ever been bred. The success rates for producing top-quality poodles are never very high. Remember that there are many breeders that have been around for years and have never produced a truly great dog. A truly great dog is one that will have a positive impact on the entire poodle breed for years far into the future or that dominated most of the shows in which it was entered, or both! A popular and realistic saying among dog breeders

asserts: "Great show dogs come in clusters—clusters of one!"

There is much more to exhibiting a poodle than just cleaning Pierre up and taking him over to a dog show and claiming a blue ribbon. Your poodle may be an excellent pet. It may also be a reasonably good representative of the poodle breed—toy, miniature, or standard. To you, your poodle may look as good as any of the dogs in the poodle books you've seen. To you, your poodle may look as good as any of the other poodles at a dog show. Unfortunately for you, however, the decision of which dog wins isn't left up to you, because you aren't the judge!

Trying to pick out which poodle puppy out of a litter will become a champion is like trying to pick out a future Nobel Prize winner, future beauty contest winner, or future Olympic gold medalist out of a group of newborn babies in a hospital nursery. To designate a pup as "show quality" is only an informed guess at best. Experienced poodle experts might put such a label on a good-looking puppy from a well-bred litter, but it would still be just a best guess.

"Pet quality" is in no way a slur on the health, the temperament, and the companion capacities of a young poodle. This pup's ears may be set a bit too high; its tail may be set a bit too low. There may be some cosmetic flaw that makes this pup a loser as a potential show dog but that certainly doesn't mean it can't be a winner as your pet poodle choice! While eliminated from exhibition for some minor defect, this poodle could have all the charm, intelligence, and devotion necessary to make it the perfect pet pick for you.

If you do decide that dog showing seems like an intriguing pastime you might like to pursue, your options are wide open. Most dog shows are good places to meet people who can help

Taking time out of a busy life to stop and smell the flowers, this toy poodle puppy is the very picture of cuteness. Puppies quickly grow up and the right owner will help them grow up the right way!

you understand what is required in the fast-paced, highly competitive world of the showing of dogs. Even if you know that you only want a poodle as a family pet, visit as many dog shows as possible to meet respected poodle breeders who may be able to help you find the right poodle for you.

Selecting a Puppy

Finding the right poodle for you and your family will depend, at least in part, on what you are seeking but, regardless of what you are seeking, don't expect any breeder to sell you the top prospect of the year. This just won't happen, especially if you are a first-time poodle owner. There are some things that you can do to help you in your quest for the right poodle:

• Study poodles. The more you know, the easier your search will be. Talk to as many poodle breeders as possible. Visit as many shows as you can. Contact the Poodle Club of America for breeders near you.

• Clearly define what you want in a poodle. Decide what size will best fit your lifestyle. Think about what you will want a poodle to do (family pet, obedience trials, perhaps retrieving). Decide if an adult dog would do as well as a puppy.

• Understand the possible pitfalls that can befall any dog buyer. Learn what paperwork should accompany any purchased puppy (see pages 37–38). Fully understand all guarantees and rights before money changes hands.

• If showing your poodle is something of sincere interest, discuss with several top poodle breeders the possibilities of becoming a part owner of a pup with show potential.

• Try to see the parents, or at the very least, the mother of any puppy that you may be considering. You may see something of what your potential choice could look like, and act like, as an adult. You may also observe the living conditions into which this puppy has been born.

• If there are several puppies that meet your general requirements as to sex, size, color, and overall quality, ask the breeder to separate these from any that are not for sale or that don't fall into the categories that you have predesignated. This will make your choice much simpler.

• Gently handle each puppy correctly, using both hands. Support the rear end and hind legs with one hand while steadying the pup's chest with the other. Make certain that you closely supervise your children if they pick up any pups.

• Watch the puppies as they interact with their littermates. Observe the way the pups are around their mother. Reinforce your own learning about pack behavior (see Pack Behavior, page 54) and the mother dog's way of maintaining control over her babies.

• Don't get all excited and pick the first puppy from the first litter you see.

A little bewildered by all the attention, these toy poodle puppies already give evidence of having good, full coats. This picture also illustrates that dilute-colored puppies, like these silvers, are born black and get lighter and lighter in color as they mature.

Arrange to see other litters to increase your awareness of what sorts of poodle puppies are available to you. You may later decide to buy that first puppy that you saw, but you should visit other litters to gain the proper perspective.

Your Poodle's Documentation

You can greatly increase your chances of getting the right poodle puppy by making sure you get the right paperwork that should go along with that puppy. You can go a long way toward getting a quality poodle and getting all the right documentation by choosing the right poodle breeder. Select a breeder with a good reputation, proven track records in dog shows, obedience trials, or the breeding of top-quality poodles.

Before you choose a poodle puppy from any source, you must be certain that the following documents are available:

• The pup's complete medication and worming records with all the correct dates.
• A health certificate, signed by the breeder's veterinarian attesting that this puppy has been examined and is healthy.
• The pup's blue AKC registration application signed by both you and the breeder. This key document is what you must send in (on time!) to the American Kennel Club to make certain your poodle is "registered." You can also give your pup its registered name on this application.
• The poodle puppy's pedigree, showing its ancestry. (This document will be only as good as the puppy source you have picked.)
• A return agreement specifying that should your plans change and you can't keep the poodle, it will be returned to the breeder rather than being disposed of in another manner

(sold, given away, euthanized, or turned over to an animal shelter). This is sometimes optional, but tells you a great deal about the quality of the breeder you have chosen.

• A spay or neuter agreement, for your signature, that assures that you will have this pet pup rendered incapable of reproducing. (This is also a good indicator that you have chosen a reputable breeder.)

If the documentation, other than the optional ones, isn't available, or if there is a promise made to send these papers in the mail, don't buy this puppy at this time! Without the blue slip, for example, your poodle may not be allowed in any AKC shows or obedience events.

Christmas Puppies

At some point you may have seen, read about, or even been a part of a cheery holiday scene with a joyful child receiving a puppy for Christmas. This scene may seem to be heartwarming, but in cold reality, it is a bad idea. Your poodle puppy deserves to be more than just one of several presents under a Christmas tree. Far too often, Christmas puppies also come as a surprise to the parents of the child who are ill-prepared for a living gift that requires a lot of care.

Puppies need to be the center of attention in order to feel welcome in their new homes. If you are contemplating giving a gift puppy, give it after the busy holidays are over. You could also give a book or video about poodles and even an announcement that a puppy would be coming after Christmas. One sensible breeder supplies an intended puppy-giver with a personalized videotape showing the newborn puppy, its mother, and its brothers and sisters. This video gives helpful hints on how to get ready for the puppy and how to treat it when it arrives. By taking this unique approach, this breeder found a way to make Christmas bright for a child without the holiday being confusing, perplexing, and frightening to the puppy.

Bringing Your Poodle Home

Bringing a new poodle puppy, or even an adult poodle, into your home for the first time can be a traumatic experience for both you and the poodle. It is also the first step in establishing the puppy or dog as a key part of your household. Be careful to make this first homecoming as free from stress as possible. Enjoy your new poodle and give it a chance to learn to enjoy being with you.

Be Prepared

The Cage/Crate/Carrier

One of the most important preparatory purchases for you to make is a cage/crate/carrier (see Crate Training, page 59). There are several versions of these canine protection/containment products that are generally lumped together under the single word, "crate." This crate should not be perceived by you, or any member of your family, as a mini-prison for solitary confinement for your new pet; the opposite is true.

Dogs, by nature, are denning animals. As such they have a great psychological yearning for a place within your environment that is uniquely theirs. An airline carrier, an enclosed crate designed for just this purpose, or one of the collapsible cages will fulfill this denning area requirement. Make this first purchase well before you bring your pooch home. Your poodle will do immeasurably better with such a manufactured den than without one. Choose a cage/crate/carrier for the *adult* size of the poodle, not for the

size it is as a puppy. You can always devise partitions to make the inside area the right current size for your new puppy as it grows.

Dishes/Bowls

Your poodle puppy will need two sturdy, not easily tipped-over dishes or bowls, one for water, one for food. Due to the amount of wear and tear these items will take, purchase items that have been designed for canine rather than human use. They should also be made of materials that can be placed in a dishwasher or, in the case of the food bowl, microwave-safe.

Your new puppy will need a number of things: a carrier, a lead, a regular collar, a training lead and collar, food and water dishes, grooming tools, some doggy toys, and the food it has been eating at its first home.

39

Children and poodles are usually a happy mixture, provided both are well-behaved! Adults should ALWAYS supervise young children when they are around pets, mostly to protect the pets!

Food

Whether your new poodle is an adult or a puppy, purchase some of the same food that the animal has been eating (see Feeding, pages 46).

Collar and Leash

A good leash (often called a "lead") and an equally good collar are necessary for your new poodle. This first collar is not the training collar (see Training Equipment for Your Puppy, page 61) you will need to teach your young poodle. This everyday collar should be the right size for an active youngster who has not yet been leash-trained. Regardless of which size poodle you have, the collar should be snug but able to slip over the dog's head with about one inch of clearance. This collar and an appropriate leash (again, depending on which size poodle you have) will allow safety and control of the puppy when you are out walking or whenever the pup is not inside your home or a fenced yard.

Grooming Equipment

Grooming equipment is necessary from the start to keep your young poodle looking good (see Grooming, pages 67) by brushing, combing, and performing the other parts of the grooming process so necessary for poodles to remain looking good. You will need a good bristled brush, a "slicker" brush (see page 73), and a comb designed for use in grooming long-haired dogs.

Toys

Most poodles need toys, both to play with and to "own." Just having some favorite playthings around will serve much the same purpose for your poodle as having a human child's security blanket or favorite stuffed animal handy.

One way to help your puppy settle in a little better is to bring some favorite belonging (loaded with the scent of its mother and littermates) from the place where the pup was born.

The Trip Home

Riding in an automobile is nothing to you, but to an eight-week-old poodle puppy it could be a terrifying experience. Other than trips to the veterinarian with its mother and siblings, your new poodle may never have been in a car before. Now it not only has to get into this strange-smelling, moving contraption, but it has to do so with people it does not know!

While it is always recommended that a traveling canine ride in a carrier for safety, the first ride home is the one exception. The puppy may need more than transportation; on this first trip it will also need some comforting. Let an adult or older (and very responsible) child hold the puppy. *Never allow a puppy or dog to ride unrestrained in an automobile!* Hopefully, the designated holder will have already spent some time with the young poodle and be considered a friend. Old clothes and an extra towel or two will help in the event of motion sickness.

Begin Training

It is important that you begin training the very minute you get home. Before you take your poodle inside to check out its new habitat, go immediately to the predesignated location you have chosen to be your pup's main "relief area." Let the puppy nose around and explore. (Some dog experts recommend "salting" this area with urine-soaked litter and some feces from the pup's original home.) You want the poodle to realize that this is the proper place to urinate and defecate. This is the first step in housebreaking your poodle (see Housebreaking, page 56). It is also one of the most important steps!

Wait patiently with your new pet. Don't pet or play with it. You want the puppy to start things off right by relieving itself at the appropriate spot of *your* choosing. When the newcomer does this at the appointed place, praise and pet the young pup enthusiastically. This should be the reward the poodle should come to expect and look forward to whenever it does what you want it to do. Establish that idea right at this spot, right now!

Note: *Never, never* scold your poodle at this important place! The relief spot is for relief, followed by reward. Don't ever confuse the poodle by reprimanding it at this place.

Introducing the Pup to Its New Home

After your puppy's introduction and rewarding at the relief spot you can take it inside to its new home. This is also a good time to introduce the cage/crate/carrier that will serve as the poodle's special place for itself inside your poodle-proofed home. After giving the puppy a chance to look around and meet the other members of your home, put the probably tired puppy in the crate, which should be located in an out-of-the-way, but not isolated area.

Poodles are not only athletic, but are a jubilant breed.

You may have placed some familiar toys and perhaps a bit of old blanket from the original home into the crate. Puppies get tired quickly. This need for a nap, combined with the comforting smells of its mother and siblings, will make the cage/crate/carrier seem less threatening. When you sense that your new canine family member is getting tired and needs a break, gently place it in the crate, shut the door, and walk away. Soon, a bright young poodle may break off contact with the others in the household when it needs to rest and go, by itself, to the quiet of its own little den.

You have another agenda for placing the tired youngster in its cage/crate/carrier. You want the puppy to associate the den with "tired" because this is where the pup is to rest and sleep. You must get this important lesson across to your new pet, for settling in is the next step in your poodle's new life with you and your family.

HOW-TO:
Poodle-Proof Your Home

Most homes are filled with poisons and other toxic chemicals that can kill an inquisitive poodle puppy. Note that baker's chocolate and antifreeze are among them. Dogs love both of them, but they can mean death.

"Poodle-proofing" your home should insure a safe environment for your poodle. Most poodles are house pets; therefore, poodle-proofing should take comfort and safety to a logical extreme.

The First Phase of Poodle-Proofing

Begin with a critical look at your entire home, especially in those places where your puppy will live or to which it will most likely have even occasional access. Look for potentially dangerous places such as:
• Stairwells, landings, and balconies from which a young puppy might jump or fall.

Puppy-proofing your home begins with getting down to a pup's level and perspective to spot dangers you might otherwise miss.

• Narrow spaces behind large appliances or heavy furniture where a pup could go and become trapped.
• Low-level vents in laundry rooms or bathrooms that could catch an inquisitive youngster's head or that might have sharp edges that could injure a puppy.
• Low cabinets that might entice a young puppy when you aren't watching. Things we sometimes keep in floor-level cabinets (cleaners, pesticides, heavy pots and pans) can kill or injure little dogs.
• Open fireplaces where a youngster could come in contact with stacked logs that could fall on it or artificial logs that could have toxic materials.
• Anything that is precariously balanced, heavy books, or a radio on a bedside table.

The Second Phase of Poodle-Proofing

This phase involves searching for all those small items—perhaps long unnoticed—that could hurt or kill an inquisitive, innocent puppy that learns by sniffing, licking, and chewing things. Some things to look for are:
• Thumbtacks, nails, pins, needles, or other tiny items that could be swallowed.

• Lead-based paint on wood in furniture, doors, walls, or baseboards.

• Pesticides, cleaners, toiletries, air fresheners, moth balls, and household chemicals.

• Furniture, rugs, draperies, and other household items that have been cleaned with chemicals that could be irritating, or even toxic, to a puppy or older poodle.

• Electrical wires, appliance cords, electrical outlets, stereo speakers, computer connections, and telephone connections.

• Sharp edges, narrow slits where a pup's head could get caught.

• Potentially poisonous houseplants (see page 87).

• Outside things like quick, easy access to busy streets, driveways, carports, or garages; de-icers, antifreeze (dogs love

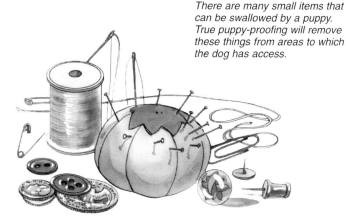

There are many small items that can be swallowed by a puppy. True puppy-proofing will remove these things from areas to which the dog has access.

the taste of antifreeze and it can be deadly to them), poisonous yard plants, fertilizers, and weed killers.

Poodle-proofing must be done carefully. It should also be done with an eye to the future growth of your poodle. Actually get down on the floor, like a puppy, and look carefully for things that could harm your new houseguest.

Helping Your Poodle Adjust

Your poodle puppy will now have to learn without the aid of its first teacher, its mother. You and your family will have to teach this pup what it needs to know to be happy and to make you happy in your home. This is an adjustment time for the puppy, but it is also an adjustment time for you and your family. It is important that each human in your household be consistent with the puppy. If you fail in this, life will only be harder for this innocent youngster.

The pup must learn that when it is placed in its den at night, it should go to sleep. You and your family must learn to let this happen! A key commandment for you and each person who shares your home is that *nobody gives in to feeling sorry for the new crying, whining puppy out there in its crate.* If anybody slips out and takes the sad baby poodle out of the crate to hug it and make it feel happy again, this person is guilty of doing real harm to the poodle. The dog must come to realize that it can't cry each time it is lonesome, bored, or just wants to be petted and loved. Dog pounds are full of dogs that never learned this lesson and whose owners lost patience with them!

First Night Blues

There are some ways to make the first few night a bit easier for the pup. You can speak to the pup with a calm and reassuring voice, but don't overdo it—you want to let the puppy know that you are close by. You can place the "smells of Mom and home" things in the crate. You could also add an old fashioned, non-leaking, hot water bottle to provide a semblance of its mother's warmth. Be sure to put the water bottle in a canvas bag that will resist the sharp, little teeth of a puppy.

Warning: Don't use an electric heating pad that might get chewed on, resulting in a fatal shock.

Some people place an old windup alarm clock with a loud ticking sound that seems to remind the pup of the heartbeat of its mother, while still others turn on a radio very low near the crate. The radio is tuned to an all-night talk radio station that seems to be helpful in putting the puppy to sleep!

The first few nights may be difficult. You and your family have already come to love this curly-haired little poodle and only want to see it happy but it doesn't seem happy there, all alone in its crate. Steel your resolve not to change the situation and your puppy will soon adjust to the crate, its sleeping time, and the absence of its mother, brothers, and sisters. If you falter now, this adjustment can take much longer and may not happen at all!

Poodles have been in close association with human beings for several hundred years. So attuned to people have poodles become that they truly thrive on people-to-poodle contact.

44

Starting Your Poodle Off Right

Your relationship with this bright, young poodle has just begun. You should remember the important role that consistency plays in your becoming a good dog owner and your poodle becoming a good pet. Properly conducted, the ownership of this poodle pup can become an extremely gratifying experience. Handled improperly, you may wish that you had never wanted a dog.

Along with consistency, shaping this malleable young dog will take time, patience, and understanding. If you add these elements to the base that you have in a fine, young poodle, and stir kindly and lovingly, following the recipe set forth by experienced poodle people, you should be able to produce a quality pet. Because poodles are fairly long-lived you may have 15 or more years with your poodle; these early days will prove to be the most significant.

The decision to get a poodle should be thought of as an investment, not something to be done impulsively, or to be taken lightly. This brown toy puppy does wish that you would include him in your considerations.

Feeding

Balance Is Everything

What you feed your poodle is going to have a direct and ongoing impact on the physical and mental health of the animal. It may also affect the dog's longevity, stamina, and personality. Feeding a balanced and consistent diet rivals training and medical care in overall importance to the well-being of your poodle.

Most important, your poodle will need a balanced diet. This means a diet that is nutritionally complete and that contains all the elements your dog will need to grow and to build strong bones, teeth, and muscles, and that thick and curly coat.

There are five important rules to follow in feeding your poodle:

1. Find a high-quality, nutritionally balanced dog food and stick with it consistently.

2. Keep plenty of clean, fresh water readily available. Water is an important part of your poodle's daily nutritional program.

3. Don't overfeed your dog either dog food or dog treats.

4. *Never* feed table scraps!

5. If you have to change foods, do so very gradually.

Special Poodle Feeding Considerations

Dogs of all breeds with long or thick coats need more nutrition to keep these coats in good shape than do most short-haired dogs. You should discuss with your poodle's breeder what was being fed to the dog to maintain a good coat. You might also ask several poodle breeders what they do. Talk with your veterinarian about the feeding requirements for your poodle's coat.

Building Blocks of Good Canine Nutrition

Good nutrition doesn't just happen. For your poodle to have a truly balanced and nutritious diet, its food must contain seven key components: proteins, carbohydrates, fats, vitamins, minerals, good drinking water, adequate owner knowledge and consistency.

Proteins

The proteins in your poodle's diet provide the necessary amino acids essential for:

- growth
- development of strong bones and proper musculature
- the ongoing maintenance of bones and muscles and their repair if they are injured.

Proteins also help combat sickness, aid in the healing process, and provide essential building blocks for the production of infection-fighting antibodies. Proteins are important in the ongoing production of the enzymes and hormones that keep chemical processes functioning.

Some sources of protein in dog foods are: poultry, usually chicken; meat items like beef and lamb; milk products; and some grains. Other sources also contribute to overall protein levels listed on your poodle's food packaging.

Carbohydrates

Along with fats, carbohydrates are one of the energy sources that fuel your poodle and keep it on the go. Measured in calories, carbohydrates in your poodle's diet are generally provided by cooked grains and other vegetable ingredients.

All quality dog foods put significant emphasis on carbohydrates. One way that a food can be designed to help control obesity in dogs is through substituting some of the proteins for additional carbohydrates. This is often seen in diets for older pets.

Fats

Another *fuel* for your poodle, fats are a much more concentrated energy source than are carbohydrates. In fact, fats provide *more than twice* as much available energy in a dog food as an equal amount of carbohydrates do. Fats are also important in transporting the key vitamins A, D, E, and K into your poodle's system. These vitamins are crucial to, among other things, helping keep your poodle's skin and thick coat healthy. Fats also help maintain a healthy canine nervous system.

As with many human foods, fats also make dog foods more palatable—or tasting better. Palatability is very important in insuring that your pet will enjoy its regular food and eat it in the proper amounts.

Vitamins

One area of canine nutrition that leads to some confusion and misunderstanding is a food's vitamin level. Generally, a high-quality, balanced dog food will contain *all* the vitamins your poodle will normally need. It is possible for a well-meaning, but underinformed pet owner to oversupplement vitamins. Unless your veterinarian suggests a specific prescription vitamin, most of the time there is no need for dietary supplementation in a dog's diet.

Dogs need lots of clean, fresh water to keep them in good condition. Never let water bowls get slimy, algae-ridden, or foul-smelling.

Minerals

Minerals play key roles in a balanced diet and are essential for the normal body functioning in your poodle. Calcium, phosphorus, and magnesium are necessary for developing and maintaining strong teeth, bones, and muscles. Sodium and potassium aid in regulating body fluids and in maintaining your poodle's nervous system. Iron in your dog's diet provides the basics for hemoglobin formation and healthy blood.

As with vitamins, if you are feeding a quality, balanced dog food, supplementation of minerals should not normally be necessary. Before you provide mineral supplements, talk to your veterinarian or to a canine nutritionist about it.

Water

There is no more important ingredient in a balanced diet than clean, fresh

The quality of your poodle's health, coat, conditioning, and general activity level will be determined in large part by the quality of the dog foods you feed it.

drinking water. Your poodle will need a ready source of water every day, provided in clean water bowls. (Water bowls should be regularly washed, with soap and warm water, thoroughly rinsed, and kept full and readily accessible.)

Gauge your poodle's water requirements on your own. You wouldn't want to drink warm, smelly water out of a slimy, dirty, algae-laden receptacle—and neither does your poodle!

Your Knowledge/Consistency

All the other building blocks for good nutrition and a balanced diet (protein, carbohydrates, fats, vitamins and minerals, and water) won't do your poodle much good without the final element— your knowledge and your consistency in feeding your pet.

Your poodle is in a closed environmental system; it must be totally dependent on you for its food. Take time to thoroughly understand just what a balanced diet is. You will want to know how to gauge the quality of a food from its label and how to feed your poodle at the different stages of its life.

Don't be swayed by clever ads, bargain deals, or fads. Don't economize on the health of your poodle by feeding a cheap, poor-quality ration. Know what you are feeding and why. Don't shift around with every breeze that blows across the pet food industry.

Sadly, some poodle owners feed whatever the convenience store has wherever they stop for gasoline, milk, or eggs. Such inconsistency will keep your poodle's digestive track in a constant adjustment phase. To test this out, look at your dog's relief spot or in your backyard. Dog feces should not be large, runny, or overly smelly. Such stools mean your pet is either sick or your dog food buying habits are sick. Talk to experienced poodle owners about what they feed. Find a high-quality, nutritionally balanced food and stay with it!

Commercial Dog Foods

There are a number of excellent dog foods available. There are also a greater number of dog foods that are just average and some foods that are mediocre at best. There are also some products that put all their operating capital into their packaging. Because dog foods are government-regulated, learning to read the required ingredient labels is one way you can do your dietary homework for the good of your pet.

Ingredient Labels

Ingredient labels are written in *descending* order. If the first ingredient is "corn," then corn makes up the highest single ingredient in the food. If

48

"chicken" is next on the list, then chicken is the second highest percentage item in the food, and so on down the list. The first three or four ingredients may make up 80 to 85 percent of most dog foods. The remaining 15 to 20 percent must include all the other ingredients that make up what your poodle would be eating in this food. If you heard somewhere that aardvark is good for your poodle (in truth, aardvark is *not* an ingredient in dog food!) and a food claims to be an "aardvark-based" dog food, if aardvark is way down the list, you know that this dog food company is playing word games on its label.

Also on the label is a list of the percentages of protein, fat, fiber, protein, and moisture. Knowing these percentages can help you choose which product will be right for your poodle's long-term feeding needs.

Premium Dog Food

There are a number of premium dog foods now available. These foods are usually somewhat more expensive and are generally found in specialty retailers, like pet products stores or feed/grain stores. Groomers, veterinarians, and boarding kennels may also carry such foods.

Types of Dog Foods

Commercial dog foods are generally made in three types: canned foods, semimoist foods, and dry foods. Each type has some unique advantages, as well as some unique disadvantages.

Canned Dog Food

The advantages of canned foods are:
• They are convenient to buy and store.
• They can be used in single meal increments (one can).
• They are highly palatable (usually due to the high moisture).

Disadvantages for canned dog foods are:
• It is an expensive way to buy dog food.
• The high moisture (as much as 80 percent) can also lead to rapid spoilage in uneaten or unrefrigerated leftovers, even at regular room temperatures.
• They are a possible contributor to loose and smelly stools.
• They can contribute (if fed exclusively) to obesity and/or dental problems.

A middle ground between the advantages and disadvantages of canned foods is the use of canned dog food in conjunction with dry dog food. Using cans as "mixers" to improve the palatability of some dry foods has worked for some dog owners and seems to be, for poodles, preferable to a straight canned diet.

Semimoist Dog Foods

Semimoist is another compromise between the convenience and palatability of cans and the cost-effectiveness of dry foods. Usually manufactured in some "meaty" shape, like burgers, semimoist foods are palatable, but not as much as canned foods. They also usually contribute to better stools than canned foods do, but not as good as those resulting from dry food feeding. Moisture percentages in semimoist foods are around 30 percent.

Semimoist foods are in-between items that can be used on trips where space may be a problem, or when your pet's interest in eating is a little down. Semimoist diets can contribute to dental problems, if fed exclusively. They are also generally fairly expensive by volume.

Dry Dog Foods

Easily the most popular form of dog food, dry dog food has many advantages. It is easy to store without refrigeration. There are many

Table scraps are just that, scraps! They have no place in your poodle's diet. Scraps throw off the balance of the poodle's regular dog food, which could be bad for the dog's health.

kinds of nutritionally balanced products in dry form. Dry food, fed exclusively, doesn't seem to contribute to tooth and gum problems to the same extent that canned and semimoist products can and stool quality is best in premium quality dry foods fed in a consistent manner.

Dry dog food's main disadvantage comes in palatability but even this disadvantage has been greatly lessened in premium foods that have sufficient fat content to make them taste much better to dogs and puppies. Dry food must also be started early in a dog's life to make it completely acceptable. Dogs fed exclusively on canned foods can be difficult to switch over to only dry foods.

Dry foods only have a moisture level of about ten percent. This makes the provision of pure, clean, fresh water all the more important if your poodle is eating a diet of dry food.

Table Scraps

Table scraps have *NO* place in your poodle's diet! Remembering the key to good nutrition is balance, how can you measure the balance in the leftovers from your table? Table scraps not only unbalance a good diet, they can be dangerous to your poodle. Small, easily splintered bones can do great harm to a dog's stomach and intestines.

Human food is generally saltier, spicier, and fattier than dog food. Obesity is one of the great killers of pet dogs (even more than Ford or Chevrolet in some places). Much canine obesity stems from the nutritionally ignorant and unwise practice of feeding table scraps. *Never feed table scraps!* You could shorten your poodle's life if you do.

Homemade Diets

As a rule, unless you can legitimately make a diet at home that fits the seven building blocks of good nutrition as well as the huge premium pet food companies can, you are kidding yourself. There may be poodle experts who can create homemade diets, but they have learned, usually over long years of trial and error, what and how much their dogs need. If you are not such an expert, your homemade diets will be more like table scraps than a nutritionally balanced dog food.

Some human foods, like chocolate, are taboo for canines, because chocolate, even in small amounts, can kill your poodle. Other foods are poorly digested by dogs and can create unnecessary gastrointestinal distress. There are hundreds of good dog food products available; certainly one of these can be right for your poodle. Discuss this with poodle-people and with veterinarians and leave dog food-making to the companies that know how to do it best!

Treats

Treats, and especially nutritionally balanced treats, can be nice little tidbits for your pet. Unfortunately, like vitamins and minerals, treats can easily be overdone. This is especially true with charming poodles who live in close contact with their humans. Some poodles are so spoiled with treats they will not eat their regular dog food. This promotes a lack of the all-important balance in a dog's nutrition level.

Treats can also contribute to the great companion canine malady—obesity. Use treats sparingly and they will mean more to the dog. Handle treats for your poodle the same way we should all handle rich desserts for ourselves!

Feeding Young Poodles (Under One Year Old)

Poodle puppies have a lot of growing to do and need the best possible nutritional start in life. Mother's milk has given them a good beginning; it is up to you to continue what she started. As with any other diet, and even more so, balance is crucial for the healthy development of a poodle puppy. Without a quality balanced diet no puppy can be expected to reach its genetic potential.

A good rule to follow is that puppies need *twice* as much complete nutrition as do mature dogs. A key puppy-feeding rule: *Unless the breeder where you bought your poodle puppy was having food problems, stay with whatever your pup was eating when you got it!*

Initially, your young poodle will need three or four meals each day. When your pup is about six months old, you can cut back to two feedings per day (which really depends on the maturational level of your individual puppy).

Puppies will need consistency more now than they will at any other time in their life. Try to feed the puppy at about the same time each day, and feed it about the same amount each time.

Feeding Adult Poodles (Over One Year Old)

Physical maturity for the three sizes of poodles occurs at somewhat differ-

ent times but, on average, adulthood is reached at about a year or a year and a half. With adult status come some new feeding requirements. The puppy food that started your poodle off should gradually be changed to an adult dog food that will be more balanced for the needs of a grown rather than a growing dog.

As with any shifts from one food to another, go about it very slowly. The poodle coat will continually need what one breeder calls "grooming from the inside." This means that the thick, curly coat of your poodle will always require a bit extra in nutrition to keep that coat full and lustrous.

If your adult poodle is involved in retrieving, obedience trials, breeding, or vigorous exercise, it may need more fats and proteins in its diet than a couch potato poodle will need. Poodles are usually active and spritely dogs, but extra activities also need to be considered when planning the dog's diet.

If your male poodle has been neutered or your female spayed (as all non-show and non-breeding poodles should be!) you will want to guard against your pet becoming too fat. This can be handled in several ways:

1. Feed the dog as if it were an older animal.

2. Be certain that your poodle gets adequate exercise.

3. Cut back on the volume of what the dog eats and eliminate most treats and certainly *all* table scraps.

Your adult poodle will still need regularity and consistency in its feeding. Don't constantly switch foods any more for an adult than you would for a puppy. Find a diet and feeding schedule that works for you and your poodle and stick with it!

Feeding Older Poodles (Eight Years Old and Older)

Older canines experience metabolic changes that require subsequent

Poodles come in a variety of sizes and colors, but all have the same happy disposition.

dietetic changes. As a dog's system slows down, energy providers in the diet will become less crucial. Many senior dog foods contain more carbohydrates than fats. There is also lower percentage protein in most senior diets.

Owner knowledge and consistency becomes more important in an older pet than in an adult. Correctly feeding an older poodle is almost as important as correctly feeding a puppy. Far too often one will hear the owner of an older and overweight poodle say something like, "Pierre always eats a full bowl of his food twice a day and has since he was a puppy." Pierre, at eight or nine, isn't a puppy anymore and food amounts need to mirror what Pierre needs, *not* what Pierre wants as far as quantity is concerned.

We have mentioned what a killer obesity is in dogs. It not only makes a dog's life more miserable, but can also shorten that dog's life! Your poodle-owning friends, your veterinarian, and your pet products retailer should be able to give you some sound advice about finding the right senior diet for your older pet.

Training

Some people envision the toy poodle as a dog meant only to be carried around. These people feel that training should be reserved for larger dogs. Nothing is further from the truth. Every dog, including every poodle, needs and deserves good training. A dog without training, regardless of its size, is an incomplete pet.

Your Poodle and Pack Behavior

It may be hard to imagine the cute toy, the energetic miniature, or the stately standard poodle as being bound by the same laws of nature that control packs of wolves or wild dogs. Pack behavior is a powerful force in the lives of any canine. This is as true for all other dog breeds and mixtures of breeds as it is for poodles.

The pack is the most important element in a dog's existence. In the wild, with wolves and other wild or feral canines, pack law controls every element of a dog's life. Each pack member has its own place in a hierarchy of other members. The pack will most often be led by the strongest, smartest male. This animal, the *alpha* male, usually gains this position by intimidating all the other members of the pack. The alpha male will hold this role until a younger, tougher, smarter, and more intimidating new leader comes along to depose him.

For your poodle, its pack must include you, each member of your household, and any other pets you may have. Under ordinary circumstances your poodle will already be conditioned for pack behavior. This happens in its brief but crucial stay with its mother and littermates. Lessons in appropriate pack behavior began for your pup even before its eyes opened. In fair, but very clear ways, a mother dog can impress a baby poodle with what things are right and wrong in its limited world. In doing this she sets the stage for your dog's training and behavior for the rest of its life.

The first thing for you to learn and understand about dog training is the key role pack behavior plays in the way a dog sees itself and others. By building on this natural form of

This silver toy poodle seems happy and content to bloom among the other flowers. Poodles will depend on their owners for everything they need. The happiest poodle is the one with an owner who understands and meets these needs.

regulated behavior training, the usually quite bright poodle is greatly aided. You and your family must fill the pack role for your poodle and *each human must be higher than the dog in the pack ranking!*

Understanding pack behavior and the significance of this support group is also important to you and to your family members. The pack is not just another "power game" to be played out at the expense of a defenseless animal. The pack is your poodle's reference point that gives your pet its sense of well-being. You or some other mature and responsible family member will have to take the role of alpha male. If one of the humans in a household won't take the job, you can be certain that the poodle itself will fill that position. Disastrous results always occur when the dog trains the family instead of the family training the dog.

Using Pack Behavior to Make Training Easier

Your poodle's mother has already initiated training. If you will follow her example, you and your poodle will have a much easier training time. Her early training was as follows:

• The mother dog always treated each member of the litter *fairly*. She did not ignore bad behavior; nor did she over-react to it.

• She punished a misbehaver *immediately*, while the pup's short attention span could connect the reprimand with the misdeed.

• She punished *without anger*, neither injuring the puppy nor continuing to scold it with barks and growls in order to modify its behavior.

• The mother dog treated her puppies in a *consistent* manner. She did not reward bad behavior one time and then punish it the next time. The fledgling minds of the young poodles soon identified Mom's displeasure with certain acts that shouldn't be repeated.

• She didn't ostracize a pup because of some bad behavior, withholding love in an attempt to gain obedience.

By using the mother dog model, your training will become greatly simplified, it will be more likely to produce the desired effect, and it will be much more enjoyable for canine and human participants. Your poodle should already understand this model and respond to it much more quickly than other training approaches.

Understanding Training Concepts

There are key things to understand about training, consistency being the most essential element. Follow these training concepts correctly and consistently and your poodle will usually be quite easy to teach:

• **Have a regular time for training each day:** Training times should be free from distractions. You can't train a pet if your full attention and that of the dog's isn't on the training. Keep your training times short (not more than 10 or 15 minutes). Keep these times devoted to the work of training and not simply extensions of playtime.

• **Remember that you are the alpha dog:** Be centered on the training. Be consistent. Keep your voice firm and businesslike. This lets your pup know that training time is different from family time, feeding time, playtime, relief walks, or any other activities. In being the alpha dog, remember the mother's example of no anger during training.

• **Set clear and reasonable training session goals:** Before you begin a training session, set clear and realistic expectations for the session. It is very easy for novice dog trainers to expect too much too soon. Handle training chores in small steps and you'll be surprised at how much you and your poodle can accomplish.

Discuss with each member of your household the lesson that you and the puppy will be working on that day. Encourage them not to confuse the youngster by later undoing the lesson it learned during the actual training session. Children can do this by using commands incorrectly or by playing inappropriately. For example, many retrievers have lost their "soft" mouths because children taught them to play tug-of-war or some other "bite and hang on" activity that had an opposite effect from that desired in the puppy.

• **Make each training session a class:** Even though your poodle will probably not need the extended rote repetitions that some breeds might require, each training time must be conducted as a class with a single goal. Don't confuse the pup with several new commands or activities.

• **Stay with one objective:** Not only are poodles usually very bright and able to learn most clearly taught lessons, they may actually get bored with constant repetition, especially with the commands they already know. While you can review previous lessons (since many commands start from ones learned earlier), it is not necessary or advisable to run through the whole list of commands before starting your young poodle on the current learning task. You should continue to praise the pup when it does well.

• **Use praise effectively:** Even though you have bonded with, and have come to love, this eager young dog, praise during training sessions is used as a reward. Always separate playtime and training time. Make sure that the enthusiastic petting the puppy gets when it correctly obeys a command is different from the hugs and fun it gets from you (or your family members) at times set aside for playing or just being together.

• **Give immediate and appropriate correction:** As in the training model provided by the poodle's mother, correction should be immediate—right on the spot. If you delay correcting your poodle for some misdeed or for some mistake in a command, you have lost the opportunity. Dogs, especially young dogs and puppies, will fail to connect the subsequent "No" with the act that made the correction necessary. It is also very important that you not use physical punishment. Striking a sensitive young poodle that only wants to please you is not only ineffective, but cruel!

• **Be patient:** Poodles are among the smartest creatures in the canine world. They are also affectionate and very anxious to please you. Even with these two positives, some poodles and some poodle trainers don't progress at the same speed. Your poodle, even with what seems to be a sometimes uncanny ability to "read your mind," is still a dog and all the training and recognition of its good qualities will not change this fact. Gauge your training with your pup's maturity and its own speed of learning. Some dogs will need extra work on a particular command, while others will catch on the first time. For best results, be patient.

• **Be smarter than your poodle:** The quickness to learn that most poodles possess is sometimes a problem for novice dog owners or amateur dog trainers. Perhaps due to their long centuries of association with human beings, poodles are quite different from a number of other dog breeds in the ease of training. This is both good and bad for you as a poodle owner. You must be sure that you are up to the job. Training a poodle may not be such a tough job in and of itself, but you can also rest assured that the poodle will learn other lessons than just those you want it to learn. Being able to structure what your pet learns and making certain that you both can recognize and undo any unwanted behavior it may learn on its own is one key to successful poodle ownership.

Housebreaking

Begin housebreaking with the knowledge that regardless of how much your poodle puppy may want your approval, on average it will have limited bladder control until it is about six months old. That does not mean that you have to wait until the middle of its first year to begin housebreaking lessons. It does mean that you can expect some accidents and that these accidents could be simply based on physical immaturity.

You can start housebreaking your new poodle the day you bring it home (see page 41). Have a selected waste elimination spot (relief area) already chosen for the youngster. Since so much of canine recognition is related to the dog's sense of smell, you might "salt" this special spot with some used litter from your poodle's previous home. The key is anticipating the puppy's need to go, taking it to the right spot, waiting until it goes, and then enthusiastically praising it for

One of the signs that a puppy needs to go outside to the relief spot is smelling around for a place to go. Another is remaining near the door.

doing what it needed to do at the place you wanted it to do it.

Crate training (see page 59) can greatly assist you not only in housebreaking your poodle, but also in having it become familiar with its new home in the safest manner possible. The cage/crate/carrier that most poodle experts recommend as a home within the home for your new pet takes advantage of innate canine behavior to keep the place in which it sleeps clean. Just as using pack behavior as an aid in training, this doggy cleanliness fetish can help you housebreak your poodle. When your poodle is in its crate it instinctually will try to hold back making a mess. If you take the poodle immediately from the crate to the relief spot outside you can use this instinct to reinforce housebreaking.

There are several key ways to help you housebreak your poodle puppy:
• Regulate the time of the puppy's meals. Young dogs only have so much room inside their bodies. Feeding them will lead to the need to evacuate waste. Drinking water will soon require a trip out to urinate. Additional pressure on the bladder or colon from eating or drinking naturally makes waste relieving a high priority for a puppy.
• Use the same relief spot (if possible). An older dog can adjust to relieving itself while out on walks with you, but a puppy needs consistency in its life.
• Use praise as a reward in all aspects of training including housebreaking. Help your poodle accumulate a mental score of many of these positive praise-rewards and the behavior that led to it being rewarded. Doing what brings praise will become almost instinctual to the dog.

Author's note: This bears repeating: *Never* punish or reprimand a puppy at the elimination location. You want the little poodle to associate going to this spot, doing what it needs to do, and then getting loads of petting and praise from the human that it adores. Don't spoil things or confuse the dog by sending mixed signals at this important place.

• In order for crate training to work, you will need to know when to remove the youngster from its crate for a pit stop. This of course comes after eating and drinking, but can also come after a prolonged period of active play, and early in the morning/late at night relief sessions.

• There are several telltale signs that a puppy needs to make a relief trip; among these are:

   1. A general look of uneasiness.

   2. Sniffing or nosing around for scent clues as to where it has gone before, which highlights the need for thorough cleaning and deodorizing of places where mistakes have occurred.

   3. Hanging around the door and looking at you as if trying to get your attention.

• If you see this warning behavior, even if the pup goes into a squat in order to relieve itself, quickly but calmly pick it up and take it out to the relief site. Even if its accident is spread from the door to the right spot, wait until the youngster defecates or urinates at the relief place and then praise it lavishly. The praise, which is one of the most important things in this puppy's young life, will help reinforce the idea that the spot is the right place to go.

• Feed a high-quality, highly digestible puppy food. The stools with this type of food (such foods are usually in a dry form) will be smaller and firmer. Smaller and firmer stools are less runny, easier for a puppy to "hold in," and easier to clean up if an accident does happen.

• *Never* feed table scraps. Not only are scraps nutritionally unbalancing but they may cause diarrhea and/or vomiting.

• Do not leave out food for your poodle puppy all day. This will make planning outside breaks impossible.

A poorly cared for poodle can be one of the saddest creatures on earth. A poodle requires a lot of love, attention, and care to reach its potential as an excellent pet.

Your baby poodle will also do much better on three or four meals each day.

• *Never* put puppy food, edible treats, or similar items in your puppy's crate. The puppy will want its refuge to be as clean as possible and food items in a crate will only cause a mess.

• Don't shift around the schedule for feeding and relief breaks. If you methodically follow the set schedule, housebreaking will become much easier.

• Don't let mistakes become repetitive by failing to adequately clean them up. Always thoroughly clean and deodorize accident spots. This keeps your puppy from picking up the false signal that this place was good once and could be used for relief again.

It is important to know that even though poodles are among the quickest dogs to become housebroken, accidents will occur. When these accidents happen there are some things that you definitely should *not* do:

• *Never* rub a puppy's nose in its own waste. This is a silly and stupid thing to do. Not only will the puppy not understand what you are doing, you'll end up with a poodle puppy in need of a bath!

• *Never* strike a puppy, for any reason, but certainly not for a biological urge that it may not even be able to control. Your puppy will consider you a god; don't bring on confusion, resentment, and fear by swatting the puppy with anything, even the proverbial rolled-up newspaper.

• *Never* use shouting as a method of puppy training. A puppy about to mess up can often be delayed by clapping your hands, which breaks its concentration. You can also use your alpha pack leader voice to say "NO" in a firm, but not overly loud manner.

• *Never* let your poodle become a nuisance by leaving its solid wastes on the sidewalk or anywhere other people may walk. Be a responsible pet owner and appropriately dispose of your pet's waste in the right receptacle.

Paper Training

A less efficient and less effective way to housebreak your poodle is to use newspapers instead of the outside relief spot. Papers, usually laid on the floor in a laundryroom or bathroom, offer a poor substitute. Some people cannot make use of the outside method that, combined with crate training, is almost foolproof with a vast majority of poodles when high-rise apartments and other living arrangements make a rapid trip to an outdoor relief spot inconvenient if not impossible. Paper training is also a possible option for people who must leave their poodle puppy for extended periods of time. The crate is certainly good for several hours, but for an entire day (which is unwise and unkind with any puppy), the less effective paper training will have to do.

Paper training involves confining the puppy to an easily cleaned area. It doesn't work particularly well with the much preferred crate training. A puppy can be easily confused when it has two relief spots, one inside and one outside.

If paper training is the only viable option, however, some key points are important to remember:

• Your puppy will need three distinct areas within the room in which you have placed it: an area for voiding waste, an area for food and water, and a sleeping area where the open-doored crate can be placed.

• The waste area should be covered with several layers of newspaper. Use only newspapers with black ink; avoid colored inks that can contain irritants to sensitive pups. Layering the papers allows you to pick up the soiled paper and leave the scent behind on the next layers to remind the pup what place to use in the future.

• Keep the relief place as far as possible from the food/water area and the sleeping area. This will keep the puppy cleaner, aid in sanitation, and make use of the natural cleanliness instinct of canines.

• Whenever appropriate, reward the puppy's use of the relief paper with praise. This praise may not be as effective as that given to the same pup at the outside spot, but the puppy still needs to know it is doing what pleases you.

• Combine the inside and outside methods by taking the young poodle out as early in the morning as possible and as late at night as possible. You might also find that you can fit in some in-between trips on weekends or on certain other days. Do so, because you will want to have your laundryroom or bathroom back when the youngster matures and can be appropriately walked outside on a regular basis.

• One method that some people use with paper training is to very gradually decrease the size of the relief area. This small area can be shifted outside, papers and all, when the puppy is old enough.

Crate Training

Crate training, unknown just a few decades ago to a majority of pet owners, is an excellent way to help your poodle become a really good housemate. The use of crate training works in housebreaking because of your puppy's natural instincts to keep its primary sleeping area as clean as possible.

Novices and non-dog-owners sometimes initially have a negative view of crates and of crate training, a view that is skewed by their general lack of understanding of two key points of innate dog behavior:

1. Dogs are naturally denning creatures. Dens give them not only a place to sleep out of the elements, but a place of their own to go when pursued, sick, injured, or in whelp.

2. Canines in the wild do not want to draw predator attention to their denning areas. Feces and urine odor is one certain way to give away a den's location and must be avoided.

Puppies are taught by their mothers that making messes in the sleeping area is a taboo. Mothers of new puppies will often eat the droppings of their newborn babies, both as a cleanliness measure and to recycle the rich milk nutrients contained therein.

In your home your poodle will want and need a place of its own. Poodles have been known to go directly to their crates in a form of self-imposed "time-out" when conditions in the house are particularly hectic. The den must always be viewed as a place of refuge for your pet, not a mini-prison. Use of the crate, not only in housebreaking, but also in general poodle ownership, can be better managed with the following hints:

• Keep a positive attitude, and encourage your family to do the same, about the cage/crate/carrier (whichever you choose to use). As with all other aspects of pet training, consistency in crate training is essential. One person in a household who sees the crate as less than positive for the poodle can undo much of the good that such a "den" can bring to the dog.

• When selecting a cage/crate/carrier, buy one based on the size that your poodle will ultimately achieve. It is true that your puppy will not need all that space at first, but eventually it will. Buy the appropriate size for the adult and then use partitions to keep the living space down to just what your pup's sleeping area will require. Too much room in a crate for a puppy may cause it to "subdivide" its area and turn extra space into a bathroom. This will destroy a key function of the crate in housebreaking.

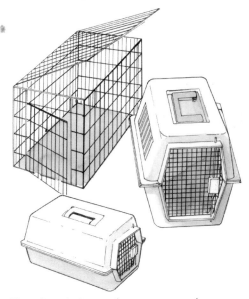

There is no better purchase you can make for your poodle than a cage, crate, or carrier that can serve as the dog's "den" or special place of its own within your home.

Can you tell if this excellent black poodle is a toy, a miniature, or a standard? The Poodle Club of America has designed the standard description for all three to be the same, except for size. The answer is in the Preface, page 5.

• Place your poodle's crate in an out-of-the-way, but certainly not isolated, location in your home. Keep the crate out of direct sunshine, direct drafts, or in other places where temperatures will fluctuate significantly.
• Place the pup in its den when it needs to rest, and for those times when you will not be able to supply adequate supervision, or when it will be in harm's way (at parties, when you are moving furniture, spring cleaning time, shopping or otherwise away for a few hours, and so forth).
• Always take the puppy *directly* outside when you let it out of the crate. When the pup performs its duties at the relief site, praise it enthusiastically.
• Don't make the mistake of making release from the crate a reward, in and of itself. Don't praise or play with the puppy (except for praise at the relief site) for ten minutes or so after it gets out of its crate. You wouldn't automatically begin a rigorous play session with your children when they come out of

their rooms; don't do this with your poodle who may become confused if it gets the "long lost child" attitude from you when it simply is brought out of its den.
• Put a sleeping mat (preferably one that is machine washable) in the appropriately-sized crate. A couple of toys can also make the den/crate more homey for a poodle puppy.
• Do not put food or water in the crate. This will only make the crate messy, which is what your pup does *not* want. Keep food and water in a regular location *outside* the crate.
• If your young poodle whines, cries, or barks in the crate, use a calm, but definitely "alpha dog" voice to quiet the pup.
• Continually reinforce the positives of the crate and of crate training to the other members of your household.
• When you are training your poodle, give it a "cool down period" in its crate right after the training session and before starting to play with the pup. This is to impress on it that training is serious business and not just an extension or prelude to play time.

When to Begin Training

Your poodle puppy may have already surprised you by quickly becoming housebroken, learning its name, and coming to you when you call. Because of their keen intelligence many poodles grasp these early pre-training lessons and fit into the household so well that further training seems a task that can wait. Don't be lulled into this kind of thinking. Now is a good time to start training. If your poodle does fairly well with the rudiments it has already received, think what kind of canine companion you can have if you go on to more specific training!

It is important to remember that there are many dog training manuals, courses, and videos available. Most of them are quite useful, but few of them are written with the poodle specifically in mind. Poodles, because of the long generations of close human contact, and because of the breed's consistent ranking in the top levels of canine intelligence testing, need a somewhat different approach than a generic one targeting all or most breeds.

Training Equipment for Your Puppy

Dog training requires some basic equipment. Poodle equipment needs will also vary because of the different sizes of the toy, miniature, and standard varieties of this breed. Discuss with your pup's breeder or with other experienced poodle-people specific equipment needs, but you will usually need:

• The misnamed "choke" collar, which shouldn't choke but which is used to restrain and remind. When you need to emphasize a training point (which isn't all that often with most bright poodles), a quick, short jerk on the leash (also called a lead) that is attached to the collar will do the job. If needed for correction, a calm, authoritative "No" can also be used in conjunction with this collar.

• The collar should be large enough to slip over your pup's head when you put the collar on but with only about an inch (2.5 cm) of clearance. Too much space between the head and the collar hampers the function of the collar by making it easy to come off. Because of the possibility of this collar catching on something, do *not* leave the training collar on your poodle at times when you are not training your pet—this collar is for training purposes *only*. Because such collars can damage the poodle's coat, many poodle owners do not require their poodle to wear any collar around the house. You will need another collar for regular use on walks and trips to the relief site, but not a training collar.

• With the training collar you will also need a training leash or lead. This

Poodles have become legendary performers in the increasingly difficult world of obedience trials. This black miniature shows off both her brightness and the poodle's heritage as a retriever.

lead can be made of leather or nylon webbing, and should measure six feet (1.8 m) long, with a swivel snap at one end for attaching to the training collar. At the other end of the lead there should be a comfortable hand loop for you to hold.

Note: Thoroughly familiarize your poodle puppy with both the collar and the lead *before* you begin training. One way to do this is to let the youngster run around, under your supervision, in an area that is fairly obstruction-free. The pup will feel the weight of the collar and the lead and become increasingly comfortable with it. Correctly done, this familiarization process will serve two purposes:

1. Your poodle will not be afraid of or apprehensive about these new things that it will have to wear; and

2. your poodle puppy will soon come to know that the presence of the training collar and training lead mean an end to other activities and a beginning of training time.

Some Additional Training Hints

Always have a proper mind set and attitude when going out to train an impressionable young dog that literally worships you. Don't try to train when you are angry or annoyed at the puppy or anything else. A perceptive poodle will pick up on the stress or tension in your voice and you may do much more harm that day than good in all the other sessions. Training an intelligent canine requires that you be prepared (read over the section on today's lesson *before* you start the lesson), equipped with the things you need, and comfortable with the puppy and yourself. If training is a chore today, *don't do it*— the pup will figure out that something about you is different and may think you are angry at something it has done!

The "sit" command uses gentle pressure to lift the dog's head while equally gentle pressure causes it to sit down. The verbal command "Sit" is given at exactly the same time the other two parts of this lesson are done.

The Five Basic Commands

These particular commands are certainly not all the commands that your poodle can learn, but they will form a foundation on which the other things can be based. Each command should be taught separately and most authorities believe each should be learned one lesson at a time before going on. Most poodles are quick learners, but what they actually learn depends on how well and how consistently they are taught. Other than common sense adjustments for the three sizes of poodles (such as taking shorter steps when teaching a toy poodle to heel than when training a standard poodle), each size can be trained following the same training methods.

Sit

The first basic command is the "sit" and should be very simple to teach your poodle since it already knows how to sit down. Your role as the trainer is to teach this young poodle to sit down when and where you want it to. This command makes a good beginning for training because it is a proper starting point and ending point for each session.

After the training collar with the lead attached is correctly in place, move your pup around until it is on your *left* and next to your left leg. Shorten the lead by taking up all but about 12 inches (30 cm) of the slack. Hold the lead in your *right* hand. In a smooth, consistent, and continuous motion, very gently but firmly pull upward on the lead at the same time you are gently pushing downward on the dog's hindquarters with your *left* hand. At precisely the same moment you are pushing downward with your *left* hand and pulling upward on the lead with your *right* hand, say "Sit" in your best, authoritarian, alpha dog voice.

Don't jerk the puppy's head up. The upward pressure is to keep the sit from becoming a belly flop and to keep the youngster in line with your left leg. Gentle and firm are important in all commands, but especially in this first lesson.

Be careful, with any of the three poodle sizes, not to use excessive force to push the youngster's rear end down. You only want to teach it to sit, not injure or frighten it. The three parts of this command work because, as the dog's head goes up, its hindquarters go down as it hears that all-important command. These must be done simultaneously for the pup to grasp all the parts of the concept of the sit.

When your pup achieves the sitting position, heap on the praise. Let this puppy know that it has done something good and that lavish praise (which the puppy craves) is its reward and that each time it does what you ask, the reward will be there. While some trainers use bits of food as a treat, the praise and your approval is really what your poodle needs. You can always praise your pet, but you may not always have bits of food handy.

Practice the sit several times more, doing each step the same way, at the same time, and in the same tone of voice. Reward the puppy after each repetition. Remember the advice given about boring the smart young poodle and keep the lesson short. Let the sit be the lesson of the week. Do it several times. At first, don't leave the pup in the sitting position for more than a minute, then gradually increase the length of time. Sooner than you think, the pup will sit when you tell it to and where you tell it to.

Stay

The "stay" is best taught after your poodle has mastered the "sit." The stay actually starts with the pup in the sitting position. Don't try to go too fast into this next command. Even though your poodle is bright, be certain that

The hand signal for the "stay" command resembles an upside-down version of the classic police signal for "stop." It is given while gently raising the dog's head and issuing the verbal command, "Stay."

sitting on command is well ingrained in its mind before going to the stay.

As with the sit command, the stay starts off on your *left* side. The pup should be calmly sitting in place by your left leg. Again the training lead will be used to keep the poodle's head up. Using your alpha voice, say "Stay" as you step away from the dog, moving your *right* foot first. At the same moment you step away, bring the palm of your *left* hand down in front of the poodle's face in an upside down form of the traditional police hand signal to stop. Be very careful to let your hand stop well in front of your pup's face to avoid unintentionally swatting the pooch in the face.

Your poodle loves you and wants, quite naturally, to be with you. The young dog may not stay in the sit/stay position very long. Be sure to praise it for any length of stay, but if the dog starts toward you, start over. The stay command goes against everything the pup really wants. Be patient. Follow the command format consistently. Your poodle will ultimately learn the stay, perhaps not as quickly as the sit, but it will stay as soon as it learns that staying is what you want it to do.

If you do have some stay problems, don't feel discouraged. Try the stay a few times and end the session with a couple of sits, rewarding the dog for sitting on cue. Leave the short sessions on a high note of praise, even if that praise is for a sit rather than for the yet-to-be-mastered stay.

Heel

Once your poodle has thoroughly learned to sit and stay, you can put some mobility into your pup's training by teaching it how to "heel." This command begins with your puppy in the sit position on your *left* side next to your left foot. You should have a strong alpha voice by now and you can use it

in conjunction with this command. The training lead, attached to the training collar, is held in your *right* hand, guided by your left hand (see the heel illustration). Using your dog's name (instead of our sample name), give the command, "Pierre, heel." As you give this command, step out, leading off with your *left* foot. If your poodle doesn't step out when you do, lightly pop the slack of the lead against the side of your leg to get its attention. Continue walking. The pup should soon get the idea.

The lead will help keep the poodle from scampering on ahead, trailing behind you, or shifting sides. You want the dog to heel at your *left* foot. Don't stop to praise the dog when it has walked a few feet in the right position. Praise for heeling correctly is given on the move and ceases when the pup stops or leaves the correct position. Praise as the reward must be given *only* when the puppy is doing what you want it to do—to walk right by your left foot.

This command must be carefully taught to a smart dog like your poodle. If the puppy stops, don't drag it all over the room or backyard. The object is not just to cover some ground, but to have your pet walk with you, stopping when you stop. The lead used with gentle pressure should *get* the dog moving. Your praise, combined with minor corrections using the lead slap against your leg, should *keep it* moving.

When you stop, give the command to sit. The "heel" isn't all that difficult because your puppy already wants to be with you. If the pup does have trouble, call for the sit and simply start over again, but be careful not to make this bright puppy resent the command by overdoing it with repetitions. As with all commands, and most aspects of your puppy's life, consistency in the way you give this command is crucial.

The purpose of the "heel" command is to get your poodle to walk with you, not ahead of you or behind you. The ultimate goal of the "heel" command is to advance to using no leash when practicing this command.

Down

"Down" can be taught after the dog has learned the "sit" and the "stay." The lead is used in a different manner this time to encourage the youngster to drop all the way down onto its belly and remain there. Instead of the upward pull used for the sit, the down requires the lead to be gently pulled straight down, thereby causing the poodle's head and chest to also go downward.

This can be best accomplished on toys and smaller miniatures by simply taking the lead in your *right* hand and pulling it downward as you make a similar movement as the one made in the stay with the *left* hand. As if you were very slowly bouncing an imaginary basketball, turn your left palm downward and move it that way in front of the dog's face as you pull down on the lead with your *right* hand. Simultaneously, give the verbal command: "Down."

As with the sit command, the pup already knows how to do the down but it doesn't know the command for it or that doing it will please you. When the puppy successfully goes down on its belly, amply reward it with the praise it wants. Don't try to force the dog to the floor or you might injure it. Be patient and your poodle will learn this command. Gradually you can lengthen the down period and even accomplish it by voice alone. At first, give praise for any length of time spent in the down position.

If you have a standard poodle, the lead might be passed under your shoe and gently pulled up to cause the larger puppy to move downward. Usually your poodle will not need too many repetitions to include the down in its repertoire.

Come

This command, the "come," may seem simple. Don't all dogs want to come to their owners? This may be

The "down" command is always done from a "sit" and "stay" position. The gentle downward pressure, the hand signal, and the verbal command "Down" are done simultaneously.

true most of the time, but you want this very important command to work *all* the time. To effectively teach this command you will need the old standby, consistency, combined with lots of enthusiasm. You should always use your dog's name with this command, as in, "Pierre, come."

When beginning this lesson with a puppy, open your arms wide and invite your loving puppy to come to you. When it does come to you, give it lots of praise as a reward.

"Come" is one command that you can "unteach" faster than you can teach it. *Never* call your puppy to you for something unpleasant, like punishment or a scolding. If you do that you can add doubt and hesitation to the dog's mind about what the outcome of obeying this command will be. Just like the relief spot where no unpleasantness is allowed toward the puppy, no one in your household can be allowed to use the come to catch the dog for something the dog doesn't like.

Teaching the poodle to come when you call should be done in an enthusiastic, cheerful manner. NEVER call the dog to you to scold or reprimand it for something. This can untrain the dog to obey this command!

If the dog has to be reprimanded or stopped from doing something *you go to the dog!* Don't spoil this important, and potentially lifesaving command by misusing it.

To maintain control over the puppy and still allow it to come to you in an unprotected area such as a city park, use a longer lead. One up to 20 feet (6.1 m) long would be good for a standard. Let the pup move around as you hold the lead. When you want it to come, give the command. If the puppy hesitates or is inattentive, give a firm, light tug followed by gently pulling the lead to get the dog moving in your direction. As with training the heel, don't drag a puppy to you to teach this command.

With smart dogs like poodles the come is one command that can be easily overdone. Don't continually call the pup to you during a lesson. This will tire the youngster and it may ignore repeated commands that don't make sense to its young mind.

The command to come can be given at odd times to effectively gauge the effectiveness of your training. While not overdoing it, call the pup from play and from other non-training activities. When it faithfully obeys you, reward the pup with lots of praise and affection.

Obedience Classes

Your poodle is very likely to excel in the basic commands, but always be patient in training a dog—your dog may be slower to mature than others of the breed, of its strain, or even of its litter! Be sure that your training style is not inconsistent or that someone in your home is not undoing the training in some way you may not know about.

If you have any difficulty at all, or if you just want to meet a lot of dog owners who have the similar goal of a well-behaved companion pet, join a class on dog training. Your poodle may be just the candidate for this type of class and your training time can be significantly shortened. Class teachers are generally knowledgeable experts and can give you dozens of hints about individualized approaches to training that can really work for you and your poodle.

These classes offer an opportunity for your poodle to become socialized, both to other humans and to other dogs. You can discuss the best groomers, the best veterinarians, the best pet products stores, and many other facts that new dog owners may need to know.

Another advantage to taking your poodle to dog school is that your instructors may be able to assess your dog's potential for further canine education. Obedience trials are excellent ways for a dog and a dog owner to take on a challenge. Your dog can earn various obedience titles and you can learn along with your dog.

Grooming

An Overview

Bathing, brushing, teeth cleaning, nail trimming—all these can help make any pet a better companion. A dirty and smelly dog isn't very pleasant to be around; the smell can permeate an entire room, or an entire house. For an inside dog like the poodle, with its dense and curly coat, good grooming is essential.

In a very real sense the poodle is a victim, and a beneficiary, of this thick coat. The coat that severely limits an ungroomed poodle is the same coat that first made it useful to duck hunters. Succeeding generations of poodle breeders built on the genetic base of the early poodle coat. When an even fuller poodle coat became a valued show attribute, poodles were chosen, at least in part, for the thickness of their hair. Gradually the poodle coat became even thicker, denser, and more in need of regular grooming.

Read and re-read the AKC poodle standard on pages 13 through 16 for information about the poodle coat, the various clips, and what dog show judges expect in the way of grooming. Even if you never expect to show your poodle, this information will still be beneficial to you.

Before You Start

Whether or not you think you want to show your poodle, you should discuss clips and coat care with a number of experienced poodle breeders and exhibitors. You should also learn about poodle coats from dog groomers, pet product retailers, and others whose expertise in this subject surpasses yours. A knowledge of poodle grooming can't be gained by reading a text on the subject any more than learning to play a musical instrument can be learned simply by reading about how to play it.

If you plan to go against conventional wisdom for beginners in this breed, and do your own grooming you will need "hands-on" training and you need to see how experienced persons handle each aspect of grooming.

Anyone with a pair of scissors or some clippers can cut all the hair off a dog but denuding a poodle takes some of the visible appeal away from the dog. Don't even contemplate being your own groomer without taking time

Many poodle breeders and exhibitors do their own grooming. Many owners of pet poodles use professional groomers, either exclusively or on an occasional basis.

Professional Groomers

Nearly all owners of pet poodles use dog groomers for some or all of their dog's grooming needs. (This is a strong recommendation for first-time poodle owners!) Most show poodle owners do much or all of their own show grooming. Grooming for a dog show is an even more precise and painstaking activity than professionally grooming a household pet. A professional dog groomer can make your new poodle an attractive addition to your home and to your lifestyle. Groomers have all the facilities to wash, clip, trim, and otherwise provide for the overall appearance of your poodle. Grooming charges vary from shop to shop depending on where you live. If you factor in grooming charges when you make your decision to buy a poodle, the costs can be budgeted and will not seem so expensive.

A reputable groomer can be a key part of your poodle's wellness team. They have a unique perspective that can be invaluable to the average poodle owner. They see your dog often enough to know it and they generally come to really care about your dog. They also see your poodle rarely enough to notice subtle changes, especially in areas of skin and coat, that may be signals of impending or existing health problems.

Ask other poodle owners about different dog groomers in your area. Let a groomer's reputation among his or her customers be a key element as you seek out the right groomer. Listen to this pet professional's opinion about your poodle. Trust a knowledgeable groomer with not only the dog's appearance, but some aspects of health as well. By weighing the groomer's ideas with those of your veterinarian and your experienced poodle breeder/friends, you can have a broad spectrum of information to use to help

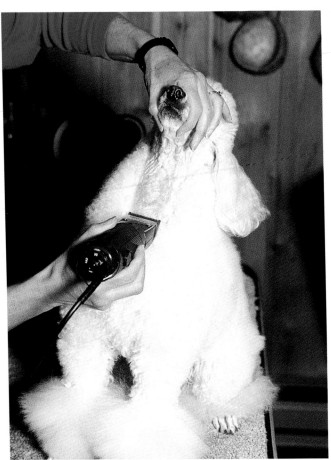

This white miniature in a puppy clip is being carefully groomed by someone who knows what they're doing with the clippers. Most pet poodles are groomed, at least part of the time, by professional groomers. A pet poodle should be fully groomed every six to eight weeks, with the owner supplying the daily brushing between visits to the groomer.

to learn what you are doing. Even to produce some of the simpler clips you will still need some training. Poodle owner, spare that poodle your trial grooming efforts. Dog grooming, especially clipping, is an intricate and precise task. Learn about it before you undertake it!

your poodle get more out of life and to help you get more out of your poodle.

Poodle Grooming Tools

Many professional groomers and poodle exhibitors have their individual ideas about how grooming should be done and what specific tools should be used to do the grooming. A general list of the bare minimum of grooming tools would include the following:
• A sturdy table with a skid-proof rubber mat.
• A bathtub or sink large enough for your poodle to be able to lie down on its side, with a skid-proof mat or surface to keep the dog from slipping or sliding around.
• Electric clippers of professional quality with several blades (#07, #10, and #15 are a good start).
• Straight scissors about 8 inches (19–20 cm) long.
• A fine-toothed and a coarse-toothed metal comb.
• A brush designed for poodle grooming with nylon bristles or wire bristles set in rubber.
• A "slicker" brush with wire bristles bent at the ends (see page 73).
• A hair dryer, preferably a dryer designed for dog grooming.
• Towels, large and small.
• Special dog shampoo and a conditioner made for use on dogs.
• A spray or spritzer to give your poodle's coat shine.

Bathing

Grooming your poodle starts with bathing. Talk to experienced poodle people and get some recommendations on what kind of shampoos and conditioners they use, and why. You want to make certain that your shampoo fits the needs of the poodle and remember, most shampoos for humans are not right for use on dogs. Some poodle colors will require shampoos that will not negatively affect them, especially the lighter colors.

One approach calls for you to wash the poodle lying on its side in a tub filled only half full with moderately warm water. Keep the dog's head out of the water and soap and water out of the dog's eyes. Put cotton in your poodle's ears to keep the water out. Let the water get over, under, around, and through the coat on both sides of the poodle.

Work up a lather, always remembering to protect the dog's eyes and ears. Don't miss any spots as you gently massage the shampoo into the curly coat. Wash first one side and then turn the dog over on its other side and do the same. Your efforts at getting the suds all the way to the dog's skin will require some elbow grease on your part.

Rinsing

As important as making sure that you thoroughly wash your poodle may be, rinsing your poodle is even more important. If you don't get all the shampoo

In the hands of an expert groomer this black standard is being shaped up. Notice that this big dog has been trained to stand patiently on the grooming table.

out of the dog's coat you can count on an unattractive poodle with skin irritations and a dull appearance. Rinsing should take you just as long as the bathing did. Rinse several times to make absolutely certain you get out all the shampoo. Thorough rinsing can be made much easier by a hand-held shower nozzle.

Conditioners

Always know the proper way to use a conditioner. It is recommended that new poodle groomers stick with products designed for dogs and not humans. With experience you may be able to use a conditioner designed for people, but stay with the products specifically for dogs until you have more grooming experience. Working with a conditioner recommended by a groomer, an experienced poodle exhibitor, or a skilled professional in a pet products store, use the product just as the directions say to use it. Don't experiment on your dog; follow the instructions.

Drying

There are several approaches to drying a poodle's curly coat. You should always start by using a thick towel to briskly dry the now washed, rinsed, and conditioned poodle. Don't speed this job along. Be thorough and towel dry each part of your poodle's anatomy.

After doing your best with a towel, you could put your poodle in its crate, which should, of course, be clean. Some poodle groomers put the dog's crate on a sunny porch and let the dog dry naturally.

Using an electric, hand-held hair dryer (unless you have access to one on a stand such as those used by professional groomers), choose a medium setting and take your time drying and brushing your poodle. Dry one part thoroughly before moving to another part. Be careful not to burn your poodle with the hair dryer by holding it too close to the dog or concentrating on one area too long at one time. Make certain that the poodle is completely dry and you will have a lot of fullness in the coat that you can now groom into any of several clips.

Poodle Clips

The Puppy Clip

The puppy clip can be worn in dog shows by poodles under one year old. This clip leaves the puppy's coat long, but the face, throat, feet, and base of the tail are shaved, with a pompon at the end of the puppy's tail. This trim presents a smooth appearance and gives the puppy a refined, consistent, and unbroken line. Minor coat flaws can be scissored into a more pleasing shape.

For many beginners, shaving an active puppy takes on near panic-attack aspects. Unless you were a barber earlier in your life, the prospect of shaving another living creature for the first time isn't a pleasant prospect. Use good judgment. Have someone—a groomer or a veteran poodle exhibitor—shave your youngster the first time. Carefully watch how the shaving is done so that you may be able do it in the future, if you really want to do so.

The English Saddle Clip

The English saddle is one of two show clips for adult poodles. It is considered one of the most intricate clips. Grooming methods are often used to help hide or de-emphasize some flaw or appearance shortcoming that a show dog may have. The English saddle clip can sometimes do just that.

The English saddle clip calls for the face, throat, feet, forelegs, and base of the tail to be shaved. Puffs are left on the front legs. The poodle tail in the English saddle clip has a pompon. The hindquarters are left with a short blanket of hair with a curved area shaved out of each flank. The hind legs have two bands that are shaved.

Most of the main coat is left full and may be shaped for a balanced appearance. The entire foot is shaved and a shaven area shows above each puff.

The English saddle, because of its degree of difficulty for novice groomers, requires some apprenticeship time to learn and some practice time to accomplish. As with all clips, if you are a new poodle owner, work with a groomer or veteran poodle exhibitor before you attempt the English saddle clip.

The Continental Clip

The other adult show clip in the United States is the continental clip. The continental calls for the face, throat, feet, and base of the tail to be shaved. The hindquarters may either be shaved bare or have a ball-like pompon covering each hip. The continental calls for all four legs to be shaved with bracelets on the back legs and puffs on the front legs. The tail also has a pompon. The foot is similar to that in the English saddle and so is the permitted trimming to complete a balanced look.

The continental is the adult show clip most often seen in American shows. It is similar to the "lion clip" often associated with the general public's perception of the poodle, especially when the pompons on the hips are foregone in favor of the full shaven hindquarters. You can learn much about the continental clip by visiting dog shows and watching exhibitors prepare their adult poodles for the show ring.

The Sporting Clip

The most utilitarian of all the show poodle clips, the sporting clip is only allowed in American Kennel Club dog shows in the special classes for stud dogs and for brood bitches. The sporting clip is also allowed in the parade of champions, where past conformation champions, now kept primarily as breeders or pets, are brought back for poodle specialty shows. As with the other clips, the face, feet, throat, and base of the tail are shaved. The rest of the poodle's coat in the sporting clip is clipped, or cut with scissors to about one inch (2.5 cm) in length and conforming to the dog's body outline. A scissored cap is left on the dog's head and the tail has the obligatory pompon.

The entire visual impact of the sporting clip is very pleasing. You can easily see the outline of the dog and the coat has a short, curly look. It is much easier to keep than other clips for

The three most popular poodle clips in the United States: Top—The puppy clip; center—The English saddle clip; bottom—The continental clip.

adult poodles, but the sporting clip retains much of that elegant poodle appearance.

The Retriever Clip

A clip that is very much like the sporting clip, but that is allowed in AKC dog shows, is the retriever clip. In the retriever clip the pompon and the scissored cap are gone. The poodle has its hair cut much shorter than in the sporting clip. The retriever clip gives the poodle a real utilitarian look. Most of the retriever clip is done with clippers (using an #04 blade). It is a good look for your standard poodle if you want the dog only as a companion. The ease of care and convenience of this clip make it popular with owners of dogs that aren't slated for the show ring.

The following items have been suggested for clipping by several experienced poodle groomers:

Clippers and Blades

There are a number of quality clipper lines on the market. There are clipper blades for every purpose. You should get some guidance from an experienced poodle exhibitor or dog

A good set of electric clippers is an excellent investment if you intend to personally groom your poodle

groomer about various brands of clippers and how they use specific blades. Different clips require different clipping approaches and different blades. Each groomer has his or her own approach, but some suggestions for the various clips are:

• The puppy clip requires no clippers, only shaving and scissoring.
• The English saddle clip is often accomplished with a #15 blade combined with scissoring and shaving. The curved places on the hips may require a #40 blade.
• The continental clip is often done using a #15 blade and also requires scissoring and shaving.
• The sporting clip is often scissored or clipped with a #10 or #07 blade that will leave about one inch (2.5 cm) of coat. Shaving is also required.
• The retriever clip can be done with a #04 blade that can radically shorten the coat.

Scissors

Never stint on the quality of your scissors (or any other grooming tool). After consulting your poodle expert, buy the best scissors that you can possibly afford. You may be able to get them at a quality pet products retailer near you. If you can't find good scissors there, visit a barber supply house. In addition to the serrated scissors recommended in your grooming kit, you may ultimately want two other kinds of scissors:

1. Straight, long-bladed scissors that come to a sharp point for general scissoring away from eyes and other sensitive areas.

2. Blunted scissors for use in areas where sharps points might be dangerous.

Handle several pairs of each scissors, much as you would try on several pairs of shoes. Find scissors that are comfortable to your thumb and fingers with a heft and feel that you can live with through many hours of grooming and trimming in the future.

As with your clippers, your scissors should be kept very sharp. Dull scissors tend to pull hair more than cut it. This makes trimming painful to your poodle and more work for you. Some pet products shops can have your scissors sharpened for you. Many dog exhibitors and regular visitors to dog shows often find several vendors offering on-the-spot scissors sharpening, repair, and refurbishment.

Just as you have to learn to correctly use clippers, you must also learn the proper way to use scissors. We all tend to think that we know how to use these things because we have used scissors for many purposes practically all our lives. This is not true for grooming scissors. The way you grip the scissors, the angle at which you hold them, the width of opening, and other factors will determine if you will do an acceptable scissoring job or butcher an innocent poodle's coat.

Brushes

The kind of brushes you choose should also be based on informed opinions from people who know how to groom a poodle. Talk with your poodle-breeding friends, with your groomer, or with a pet expert at a pet products store. These sources will help you not only find the right kind of brushes but the best buys on these brushes. Many groomers of show dogs pick a brush with bristles or with metal pins with blunted ends to avoid hurting the poodle's skin. The bristles or the pins should be mounted in a rubber platen that not only cushions the bristles or pins but also allows them to bend a bit as they are pulled through a dense part of the poodle's coat. Again, it is important to buy the very best quality brushes for the sake of the poodle and for the sake of your purse or pocket.

You will need a good "slicker" brush to remove old, dead hair and bring out the lustre in a poodle's coat.

Better brushes also last much longer than do cheaper ones!

A second type of brush, which is actually more in use with pet poodles, is the slicker. Slickers have fairly fine, bent, wire tines mounted in very close rows. They are very helpful in removing mats. The slicker brush, which should be bought with the size of your poodle in mind, can also help get out old, dead hair that can take a lot of the luster from a poodle's coat.

Combs

Much of your home grooming for your poodle will involve brushes and slickers but you may also need a quality grooming comb. Buy what you have seen in the hands of poodle experts and groomers who have had success with keeping poodles' coats presentable. As with clippers and brushes, combs need to be of the very top quality.

Tables and Other Grooming Items

Whether your poodle is a very small toy, a little bigger miniature, or a very big standard, the use of a grooming table is always recommended. As with so many other facets of grooming (and poodle ownership in general), the earlier a puppy accepts and becomes comfortable on the grooming table, the easier and more effective your grooming efforts will be.

Many poodle breeders and exhibitors like portable, folding grooming tables that may be stored out of the way when not in use. It is important not to sacrifice strength and sturdiness for portability. A wobbly table that frightens the poodle with its lack of stability can make grooming dangerous and unnecessarily difficult. Choose a table that will serve as a solid platform, with a non-slip surface. Both you and your poodle will be more comfortable, especially when you must perform those tricky trimmings around eyes, ears, and other sensitive areas.

Make sure that the table, if not equipped with height adjusters, is at a level at which you can comfortably work. Try out several sizes and heights to give yourself an idea of what your specific requirements are. Get a table with widespread legs that will help prevent turning over. Also make sure that the place you choose to place this table has a level floor.

Restraints. Even though most poodles are trained to stand still on a grooming table, restraints are good accessories. These devices, usually in a hammock or sling design, fasten to the table and provide added stability to your poodle by keeping its body in place when both your hands are busy grooming. Another form of restraint, also attached to the table, is a collar/short leash arrangement called a grooming loop. This thin, soft leather (or nylon) loop is very flexible and fits over the poodle's head and around its neck. Because it is attached to an upside down "L" post, which is in turn fastened to the grooming table, the poodle is made to stand still and is unable to move off the table.

Dryers

It is possible for you to towel dry your poodle and then put the dog in its cage/crate/carrier for a session of natural drying but most poodle groomers use an electric air dryer to dry the dog more thoroughly and to give the poodle a neater, more coiffured look. There are many types of dryers than can handle the job of removing the dampness from your poodle's dense ringlets. While professional groomers and show dog owners usually use large dryers manufactured especially for heavy duty use, the pet poodle owner can possibly get by without the expense by using a regular dryer intended for human use. It is important, especially in your and your poodle's first grooming interludes, that the dryer setting isn't too hot and that you don't hold it too close. If you hurt a puppy by careless use of a dryer, the pet may long remember and fear the dryer.

It is important to remember that shaving, scissoring, and clipping all require some skill, some experience, and some manual dexterity. Unless you are careful you could scrape, cut, or clipper burn your poodle. No apologies are necessary for encouraging you to serve an apprenticeship with someone who really knows how to accomplish the visual miracles that occur when a good poodle is correctly groomed.

Groom Early and Often

Your poodle puppy will need to be carefully and consistently groomed throughout its entire life. Start the youngster early to get it accustomed to the sounds and feels of grooming. Gradually introduce your young puppy to the whirring monster that humans recognize as a clipper. Don't frighten your poodle with the clipper or you may always have a real chore when grooming time come around.

Grooming, especially the regular brushing that is sufficient for most pet poodles, can be a positive experience for you and the dog. For a young poodle, a thorough combing and brushing is usually sufficient. Don't leave any matted or tangled places or the next time you brush your poodle will likely be a difficult session for you, and a painful one for your poodle.

Brush your poodle puppy's hair in the opposite direction from the way it grows. Do this without tugging or hard pulling and soon, with continued brushing, the coat will be smooth and flexible and will easily yield to the brush. Finish the session with a thorough combing with a coarse comb and then follow up with a fine comb.

An adult poodle is first brushed the way the coat is growing and then against the way the coat grows. Follow with a thorough coarse combing completed by a thorough fine combing. Start at the poodle's head and go down its neck onto its back, and then onto its tail. You then brush and comb down each side to the legs. Go on to the head and the ears, leaving the tail for last.

Because the poodle coat needs at least weekly attention to look its best, even as a pet, set a regular time for bathing, drying, brushing and the other facets of nail trimming, teeth cleaning, and ear checking that will complete your poodle's grooming routine.

Indirect Factors Affecting Grooming

Poodle coats don't just happen. The development of a quality coat in even a pet poodle calls for an environment that will be conducive to the development of this coat. This environment begins with the right diet. Your poodle must expend a certain amount of the nutrition it gains from the food it eats to produce a better than average coat. You cannot achieve excellent results feeding a mediocre dog food. Your poodle has extra needs brought about by the coat requirements that short-haired dogs don't have. Feed a quality food that has sufficient protein and fat levels (see Feeding, page 46) to give your dog the extra fuel it needs for this purpose.

Another indirect factor is the cleanliness of your poodle's home. If your poodle is an outside dog most of the time, it will have different needs. The sun can bleach a dog's dark coat, yellow its white coat, and burn a dog's skin. Exposure to different types of soil can stain a coat, which can require a more concerted grooming effort.

If you allow your poodle to become flea-infested its coat will definitely suffer. The same is true of ticks. Tick scars on places where a poodle is shaved to the skin are unsightly. Keep your poodle away from these parasites (see the following chapter, Medical Care). The same is also true for timely treatment of mange and other skin problems. A mangy dog of any sort is a sorry sight to see; a mangy poodle is sadder still because the dog so depends on its appearance as a breed characteristic.

Medical Care

Keeping Your Poodle in Good Health

Common sense is the centerpiece of any plan to keep your poodle healthy, but it can be enhanced by several recommendations:

• Avoid locations, situations, and conditions where there is a danger of potential injury or infection.

• Follow a careful regimen of a nutritionally balanced diet, lots of clean, fresh water, and regular exercise on a daily basis.

• Be parasite-conscious and keep your poodle as free as possible from these health-robbing pests.

• Maintain a safety-first attitude by assuming that the worst can indeed happen; always use a leash outside fenced areas, and *NEVER* leave your dog in a parked car even on a moderately warm day.

• Establish and maintain a regular schedule of visits to your poodle's veterinarian for checkups and ongoing preventive health care.

The Health Team Concept

You and your family will most obviously be key members of your poodle's health team. As primary members who are around the dog every day, you will be responsible for maintaining a safe environment, providing the right foods, and seeing to it that your dog has appropriate exercise. You also must arrange regular medical visits.

Your veterinarian will be the next member of this team. A veterinarian will help your new poodle get off to a good start, nurture it through the days of its adulthood, and provide care in its senior years. A key to the best use of this important resource is to visit the veterinarian *before* problems arise, not only in medical emergencies.

Another significant member of your dog's health team should be an experienced poodle person whose background with the breed will be an invaluable asset. This knowledgeable friend can add perspective to your poodle's health needs by seeing the dog often enough to know it, yet infrequently enough to spot subtle changes that you might miss in your day-to-day contact with your pet.

Essential on any poodle health team is a reliable dog groomer. Each time your poodle is groomed, an alert, professional groomer can give you valuable information about small, but important aspects of your poodle's development and overall health. Groomers can spot changes in skin conditions and hair quality, small injuries, parasites, and a myriad of other things that other team members may overlook.

Preventive Care

Regular visits to the veterinarian will provide an early warning of impending or potential health concerns. These scheduled checkups will also alert you to existing conditions that should be treated. Your veterinarian will keep your poodle current on its immunizations, which are often required by law, as well as by your desire to have the healthiest poodle possible. Where you buy your poodle puppy can often be the single greatest factor in how many health concerns you will have to face in the life of your pet. Getting a poodle from sound, healthy stock that is as free as possible from inherited conditions and defects won't guarantee an illness-free pet, but it can greatly increase your chances of getting one!

Combine wise choosing of a poodle with regular veterinary visits, a quality and balanced diet, and consistent care. Add to this prevention prescription a proactive attitude about avoiding possible disease and injury and your poodle will have a much better chance of being the pet you want, because you have become the owner it needs.

Immunizations

The first line of defense for disease prevention is a well-designed immunization program. Your poodle should have received its first round of these protective inoculations even before it came to live with you. Because you were wise in your choice of a source for this pup, you will be able to get a record of what immunizations the youngster had while still at the breeder's. The veterinarian that you picked out to be your poodle's dog doctor and friend will be able to continue what your pup's first owner began.

Initial shots include the first salvo of inoculations against distemper, parvovirus, hepatitis, leptospirosis, parainfluenza, coronavirus, and *bordetella*. Your pup should have received the first round of these shots at six weeks of age. Other shots are usually given at eight to ten weeks, and still others at twelve weeks of age.

With the assistance of your veterinarian you can develop an immunization calendar for your young poodle. This calendar should have pre-set dates and appointments for these important safeguards against disease.

Diseases Controlled by Immunizations

Distemper: Distemper was once one of the most dreaded diseases that a puppy or an entire kennel could encounter. Widespread, highly contagious, and often fatal, distemper could strike and wipe out all the unprotected puppies and most of the young adults in an entire dog breeding facility. It still can. The answer is immunization.

Canine distemper is a viral disease that can be observed as soon as a week after exposure to an infected animal. It can be characterized by a number of symptoms, but often distemper would initially seem to be nothing more than a cold with a fever and nasal discharge. The youngster with distemper would appear listless and tired; it would lose its appetite; diarrhea would often be present.

Old-time dog breeders referred to distemper as "hard pad" or "hard pad disease" because of the toughening and rigidity often seen in the toe, foot, and nose pads of the affected animal that developed weeks after the initial signs of infection were noticed. Distemper would often have a cruel, delayed twist. Its victims would appear to have conquered this canine killer and then it would break through again. The latter stages of this dread illness would bring spasms, convulsions, paralysis, and finally death.

Modern veterinary medicine has a preventive against distemper that has greatly reduced the incidence of this killer. This immunization is included in the regular round of inoculations that your poodle puppy should have.

Rabies: The very mention of rabies can still bring a chill to most people. Visions of pet dogs turned into raving monsters with foaming mouths were, and still are, the stuff of nightmares.

Unfortunately, rabies is no dream-state illusion—it still exists in much of the world and could come in contact with your poodle and you!

Most poodles are house pets living in the homes of their owners. This does not negate the need for ongoing rabies vaccinations for your poodle. Any warm-blooded animal can be a potential rabies carrier: a stray dog, an alley cat, or a raccoon. If unprotected against rabies, a minor nip from a carrier can make your best friend into a potentially deadly enemy who can transmit rabies to you! It is still widespread in some parts of the United States.

Rabies can take on two manifestations. One of these is the "mad" dog, or "furious" version, where the infected animal ferociously attacks just about anything around it—other animals, humans, even trees or automobiles. The second rabies form is the "dumb" form, which is more lethargic. In this "dumb" type of rabies the dog is listless and slowly drifts into a coma. In both expressions of rabies, a fear or avoidance of water gives rabies another name, *hydrophobia*.

Leptospirosis: Leptospirosis is a bacterial disease that normally affects an animal's kidneys. Commonly spread by drinking water that is contaminated by the urine of an infected mammal, leptospirosis can, in severe cases, damage not only the kidneys, but also the liver. Sores can appear in the dog's mouth and weight loss can be present, along with a weakening of the dog's hips and back legs.

Symptoms of leptospirosis include: loss of appetite, diarrhea, vomiting, fever, and abdominal pain. Your poodle can be safeguarded from leptospirosis by initial immunization followed by annual booster shots. Humans are also susceptible to leptospirosis.

Hepatitis: Infectious canine hepatitis is a different ailment from the hepatitis in humans, but it can affect any member of the dog family. It ranges in degree of severity from a deadly viral infection that can prove fatal within 24 hours after it is diagnosed, to a fairly mild, inapparent form that may even go unnoticed.

Hepatitis is spread by urine or feces from an infected animal. Clinical signs of the illness are fever, listlessness, abdominal pain, tonsillitis, sensitivity to light, and blood in the dog's feces or vomitus. Prevention comes from initial immunizations and annual booster injections.

Parvovirus: Parvovirus is an especially tough killer of very young puppies, but it can be fatal (in an unimmunized dog) at any time of a dog's life. Parvovirus primarily attacks a canine's immune system, gastrointestinal tract, heart, and bone marrow. Puppies nearly always suffer from severe dehydration brought on by heavy diarrhea and vomiting, in which blood is often present.

Parvovirus is a quick and deadly ailment that can kill a young dog or puppy in as little as two days. While some pets can be saved from parvovirus by immediate veterinary care, the best way to keep parvovirus away from your poodle is through an effective immunization strategy, backed up by ongoing annual shots.

Parainfluenza: Parainfluenza is believed to be spread by contact not only with infected animals, but also by particles expelled in breathing and coughing from dogs with the disease. Highly contagious, parainfluenza can spread through an entire household, affecting several dogs or an entire litter of puppies. Parainfluenza is one of the causes of tracheobronchitis, identified by a characteristic dry, hacking cough followed by repeated attempts to dispel or cough up mucous.

While not a dreaded killer in and of itself, parainfluenza can seriously weaken a dog or puppy to the extent that it is left highly vulnerable to other infections and diseases. Isolation is one way to slow the spread of parainfluenza, but the wisest course is initial and ongoing immunizations.

Coronavirus: Dogs of all ages can become victims of this contagious disease. Clinical signs of coronavirus infection can vary from soft and loose stools to severe diarrhea with very foul-smelling and watery stools tinged with blood. Occasionally, there is also vomiting.

Treatment can be successful, but like parainfluenza, coronavirus can leave an affected pet in a weakened state and open to attack by other ailments. Even though treatment is possible, immunization against this virus is the best thing for your poodle.

Bordetella: This bacteria is part of the tracheobronchitis complex. Bordetella is the most common bacteria isolated from dogs afflicted with tracheobronchitis. It is often part of the most serious tracheobronchitis form, bacterial bronchopneumonia. The parainfluenza immunization can usually keep both Bordetella and tracheobronchitis at bay.

Borelliosis (Lyme disease): This tick-borne disease affects many mammals, including humans. Medically termed borelliosis, Lyme disease is now often referred to as Lyme Arthritis in human beings. This is a serious and potentially fatal ailment spread by the tiny deer tick (and potentially by other ticks as well). It is through contact with tick-infested areas that both dogs and humans can come into contact with this disease.

First identified in Lyme, Connecticut, borelliosis has now spread to all parts of the continental United States. Once only a disease seen largely in outdoor activity enthusiasts, borelliosis now has invaded suburban areas and even some city parks and recreation areas.

It is possible that walking your poodle in any shrubbed or wooded areas could expose your dog and you to the carrier ticks.

Clinical signals of Lyme disease include tenderness around joints accompanied by swelling, and may include a loss of appetite as one of its signs. If you or your poodle are bitten by any kind of tick, you should seek professional attention as soon as possible. Have all ticks found on your dog or you identified by medical or veterinary personnel even if there have been no tick bites. Borelliosis is now thought to be more serious for humans than it is for dogs. Take no chances if you are bitten by a tick of any sort!

Parasites

External Parasites

Fleas: The curse of many dogs' lives, fleas are the most common parasite affecting dogs. Like little vampires, fleas feed on your dog's blood and can cause anemia if the infestation is severe enough. Fleas are also hosts for another parasite, this one an internal pest, the tapeworm.

Occasionally, a dog will develop a quite severe allergic reaction to fleas. Flea-bite allergy can make your poodle absolutely miserable. This reaction causes severe scratching, hair loss, and much discomfort to the affected dog. Flea-bite allergy requires immediate veterinary diagnosis and care. The second phase of this confrontation means you have to banish fleas from your pet's life and lifestyle.

Show fleas no mercy! You must understand that fleas are among the worst parasitic enemies your dog has. The dog has no way to rid itself of these serious pests and must depend on you. Eradicating fleas from your poodle's environment means engaging in all-out war against them. If your dog has fleas, they can be everywhere your dog goes. This will include your house, your yard, your car, your dog's kennel—anywhere that the dog can get to or visits. You can de-flea most of these areas or even all but one of these areas and still have failed because the fleas will have left eggs and pupae in that one remaining spot and start up again from there.

Talk with your veterinarian and with other animal care specialists about the right weapons to use against fleas. Dips, shampoos, flea collars, dusts, and sprays are available. Foggers, house sprays, carpet dusts and cleaners, and traps can all be used in your home or car. Kennel sprays and yard treatments are designed for outdoor areas such as your backyard. Also remember to treat any occasional places your dog may visit, such as your cottage at the lake.

Fleas spend 90 percent of their life cycle off the dog. It is the adult fleas, which make up about one tenth of the total fleas in an area of infestation, that will actually be on your poodle. Treating only the small portion on the dog and leaving the others to hatch, mature, and reproduce is a waste of time.

Ticks: Ticks are much larger bloodsuckers than fleas, but getting rid of them isn't quite so difficult. Many of the treatments and deterrents used for fleas will also work for ticks. For dogs, such as poodles, that may be groomed with some of their skin left showing, ticks can be an additional problem. Tick bites, and the incorrect removal of ticks, can cause infections and unsightly scarring that can detract from a poodle's appearance.

Ticks can also bite humans. They sometimes carry serious, life-threatening diseases, such as Rocky Mountain Spotted Fever and Lyme Arthritis (see Borelliosis, page 79). Ticks require diligence on the part of a poodle's owner, but they don't usually involve the same widespread, lingering infestations that fleas do. It is a good idea to regularly inspect your poodle after you have been anywhere ticks may be. The tight poodle coat can help keep ticks from getting through to the skin, but it can also hide the ones that do get to the skin. Check the entire dog carefully, especially in tick favorite locations like the ears, face, and neck.

Ear mites: Poodles can be susceptible to ear mites, another external pest that can make life miserable for your dog. These tiny pests inhabit the ear and the ear canal. A dark, dirty, waxy residue in the ears can signal an ear mite infestation. You can also tell that these microscopic pests are around by observing your poodle. If your dog vigorously shakes its head from side to side, or if it constantly paws at its ears, ear mites are a good possibility. Follow your veterinarian's recommendations as to treatment and eradication of these parasites. When you perform your regular checks of your poodle's ears, always look for signs of the presence of ear mites.

Mange: There are two kinds of mange, both kinds caused by mites:

1. *Demodectic* or what was once called "red" mange is a special problem seen in very young and very old dogs. Demodectic mange can cause very rough and patchy areas around the head, face, and eyes, and in other places on an afflicted animal's body. Sometimes this version of mange can cause widespread hair loss and severe, painful itching.

2. *Sarcoptic mange* owes its presence to another mite that burrows into your dog's skin. It often causes severe hair loss and itching that can cause a dog to scratch itself raw. Sarcoptic mange has another side effect—it can also be transmitted to and from humans. On people it is usually short-lived, but it can cause itching and a rash.

There are dozens of suggested home remedies for both kinds of mange, but you should always consult your veterinarian. Follow this professional's advice both in treatment and in prevention of these ugly, uncomfortable, parasitic conditions.

Just because your poodle is predominantly a housedog, don't become complacent about external parasites. Rats, mice, and squirrels can bring these problems right into your backyard or onto your deck, balcony, or patio. Walks in the park, a country outing, or even a relief trip outside could expose your poodle to these pests whose lives depend on parasitically living off your pet.

Internal Parasites

Roundworms: Roundworms attack the health and vitality of dogs of any age. Puppies are especially vulnerable to them and may have had them introduced into their bodies even before the puppies were whelped. If a mother dog has roundworms she can pass them on to her litter.

Roundworms drain away the strength, vigor, and even physical potential of puppies. Youngsters with roundworms will simply not grow and flourish with these internal pests present in their bodies. It is difficult enough for pups to gain the health and nutrition they need to reach their potential as mature dogs without having to share their health with a group of parasitic interlopers.

Consult with your veterinarian early in your poodle puppy's time with you. This professional can ascertain if your dog has roundworms and then recommend a plan of action to dispel them. One sign of roundworms is their presence in either a dog's stools or in its vomitus. Other signs of roundworms could include rough coats, pot bellies, and poor overall appearance.

An elegant apricot miniature with a look of serene alertness, perhaps anticipating entering the show ring. Well-groomed, healthy, and well-bred, this poodle may be one of that tiny fraction of all poodles that is truly worthy of being used for breeding.

Maintaining a clean environment will greatly aid you in keeping roundworms and other pests away from your poodle. Always quickly and appropriately dispose of stools. Use appropriate sanitary measures to keep worms from getting a start with your dog. It is wise to remember that children and other humans can also become infested with roundworms.

Hookworms: As with roundworms, hookworms can affect dogs at any time of their lives. Puppies that are struggling to grow are again especially at danger from hookworms. Hookworms attach themselves like tiny lamprey eels to the inside of a youngster's small intestines. These parasites thrive on the blood they siphon off from the host animal, greatly weakening the pup's ability to withstand disease and infection.

Clinical signs of hookworms are bloody or tarlike stools. Your veterinarian can finish off the hookworms before they do something that could lead to more serious health problems for your poodle. Consult your veterinarian and then follow what this professional recommends.

Tapeworms: Fleas introduce tapeworm larvae into a dog's system. A tapeworm-infested poodle will not become the family pet that it could become; tapeworms, like other parasites, will take away part of a dog or puppy's physical reserves.

As with other parasites, the clearest course of action involves your veterinarian. Let the veterinarian advise you both on overcoming tapeworms and

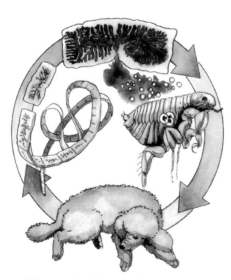

Fleas can be infested with a parasite themselves—the tapeworm that is passed on to your poodle when it swallows a flea. Another reason for making your dog and environment flea free!

on overcoming their delivery system, the flea.

Heartworms: Along with the tapeworm, the heartworm is an unwelcome gift from an unwelcome pest; however, instead of the flea serving as host for the parasite, infected mosquitoes can introduce the heartworm into your poodle. Heartworms were once a regional problem, but today much of the United States is on alert for these potential killers.

The heartworm gets into your pet's bloodstream through the bite of a mosquito that is a carrier for this parasite. Once inside your poodle, heartworm larvae travel to the heart. Unless they are stopped by medication or treatment, the heartworms will literally clog up a dog's heart. Death is almost always certain in untreated animals.

Veterinary medicine has produced a preventive that must be given on a regular basis to keep heartworms away from your pet's heart and ultimately prolong its life. If not prevented in young adult animals, an expensive and possibly dangerous treatment is possible. With heartworms, the prevention is much simpler than the treatment. Treatment is much more kinder than letting a heartworm-infested pet die needlessly.

Other Medical Problems

Poodles, like dogs of all other breeds, are targets for other health problems. Because a poodle usually spends a lot of time in close contact with its human family, some of these health problems will be easier to observe.

Anal Sac Impaction

The anal glands are on either side inside of the dog's anus. In the normal stretching and contracting during bowel movements, these glands are usually emptied of the foul-smelling secretions that collect there. If these glands become clogged or impacted, they cause a dog a great deal of discomfort and may have to be emptied by hand.

If you see your poodle dragging its rear end along the floor in a "scooting" motion, impacted anal glands are a possible reason. Your veterinarian can easily teach you how to empty these glands or will do it for you. Don't let this common condition cause your pet unnecessary discomfort; pay attention to the anal glands!

Diarrhea

Most dogs will suffer from diarrhea at some times in their lives. Stress, rapid dietetic changes, or internal parasites can be common causes of diarrhea. While this condition is not usually serious, diarrhea can be a clinical signal of the beginnings of some serious ailment. Any diarrhea that continues for more than 12 to 24 hours, or that has traces of blood in the resultant stools, merits a visit to the veterinarian.

Vomiting

Vomiting, like diarrhea, is a fairly common canine occurrence. In puppies, too much excitement after eating can bring it on. Changes in diet and stress are also usual causes of ordinary vomiting. As with diarrhea, vomiting may be a sign of some more serious illness or condition. Combined with diarrhea, vomiting can rapidly put a pup in serious shape from dehydration. Vomiting that lasts longer than 12 hours deserves a trip to the veterinarian.

Bloat

Bloat, or gastric torsion, is one of the most serious conditions for dogs. Usually affecting deep-chested dogs, which will include standard poodles (rarely toys and miniatures), bloat affects enough poodles to encourage all poodle owners to play it safe and

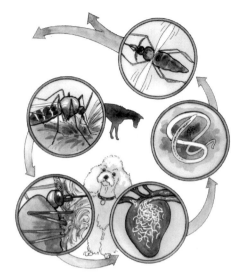

Mosquitos pass on heartworm larva from other animals already infected with heartworms. Untreated, these larva grow and can nearly clog a dog's heart, causing a lot of suffering and eventual death.

become familiar with bloat. Bloat can destroy the life of an otherwise healthy and happy poodle in just a few hours. It involves a swelling and twisting of a dog's stomach from water, gas, or a combination of the two.

Bloat and its causes are still somewhat of a medical mystery. There is a list of what might cause a dog to bloat; it is believed that some of these suggested reasons can evidently bring about bloat independently or can work in conjunction with other reasons. Some suggested causes are:
• A genetic predisposition in some breeds and in some families (or strains) within these breeds.
• Intense stress from any number of sources.
• Strenuous exercise following a large meal (particularly of dry dog food) and the intake of a large amount of water.

Ever alert, this young black standard poodle illustrates the largest poodle variety.

• Excessive salivation and rapid breathing.
• Pale and cool-to-the-touch gums and skin in the mouth.
• A shocked or dazed appearance.
• Repeated tries at vomiting without producing any vomitus.

To have any chance at saving the life of a dog with gastric torsion, you must act immediately. Call your veterinarian and alert him/her of the possibility of bloat. Safely, but with all urgency, transport your poodle to the animal clinic.

Special Health Concerns for Poodles

Some of the special health conditions afflicting poodles are rare; others are more common; many have a genetic or inheritable beginning. If you know of, or suspect, any of these disorders or abnormalities in your poodle's background, discuss them with poodle experts and consult a veterinarian for a complete checkup and recommended treatment methods.

Addison's Disease: This deficiency in adrenocortical hormones shows the common clinical signals of: diarrhea, vomiting, overall lack of strength, general lack of good physical condition.

Epilepsy: The same neurological disorder that afflicts some humans, epilepsy can be recognized by seizures or convulsions when irregular electrical discharges to the brain are received. Epilepsy can be controlled through medication. Consult your veterinarian.

Hypothyroidism: This disorder stems from low hormone production levels in the thyroid. Clinical signs include: irregular heart beats, skin and coat problems, obesity, a lack of mental acuity, and a lack of energy. Hypothyroidism can be treated by prescription medicines.

Legg-Calve'-Perthes: This condition is caused by the deterioration of the upper parts of the femur that can

• The age of the dog; dogs over 24 months of age seem to be more likely to bloat than younger animals.
• The sex of the dog; males seem to be more affected by bloat than females.

Whatever the reasons or causes for bloat, gastric torsion is a real killer of dogs among the deep-chested breeds. While your poodle will probably not be as high on a list of bloat candidates as a bloodhound or Great Dane might be, don't take chances on this dreaded condition.

Some clinical signs of bloat are:
• Obvious abdominal pain and noticeable swelling in the abdominal area.

result in lameness in some toy poodles. This can be a fairly painful condition; some dogs get over it and others require surgery.

Patellar luxation: This is a weakness of the kneecap in toy poodles that can be repaired surgically. The kneecap slips out of position and causes some temporary lameness in the leg.

PRA or Progressive Retinal Atrophy: PRA is an illness in which the light cells of the retina don't receive enough blood. As a result, these cells gradually deteriorate, causing blindness. This is a serious problem affecting some families of poodles, Irish setters, and other breeds. Because PRA can be identified by a veterinarian specially trained in diseases of the eye, the American College of Veterinary Ophthalmologists, through the Canine Eye Registration Foundation, has developed a registry and certification process to insure that poodles, and dogs of other breeds, are annually certified as clear of PRA and other inheritable eye diseases.

Sebaceous adenitis: Hair loss, a type of dandruff-like flaky skin, and smelly skin infections are all clinical signs of sebaceous adenitis. This chronic skin condition is brought about by irritated, often abnormal sebaceous glands. Antibiotics and regular bathing in special medicinal solutions may bring this disorder under control, but SA is also thought to be inheritable. Poodles with this ailment should not be allowed to reproduce and spread this condition on to successive generations.

Note: The PCA has established a special research fund to research SA, especially in standard poodles.

Von Willebrand's disease: This inherited, hemophilia-like blood disorder stems from an abnormality in the dog's blood. Free bleeding is a key clinical symptom.

Canine hip dysplasia or CHD: This is a medical condition in which the hip

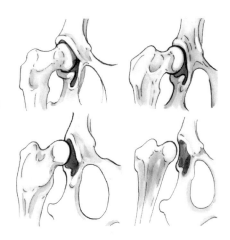

A visual explanation of hip dysplasia: Top left—a normal hip and normal femur; top right—some partial dislocation (subluxation); bottom left—acetabulum (socket) is shallow and subluxation is present; bottom right—luxation (dislocation) is present, head of the femur is flattened.

joint is slack or loose. This slackness or looseness is combined with a deformity of the socket of the hip and the ball-like femoral head joining the thighbone. This malformation of the development of the hip and the connective tissues results in an unstable hip joint with an unsteady, wobbly gait that is clearly painful to the dog.

While poodles are not the highest in numbers of dogs with CHD, and then only in standard poodles, and while CHD is not clearly always caused by inherited genes, a wise poodle buyer would do well to be certain that the parents of a prospective puppy are free of this disorder. The Orthopedic Foundation for Animals (OFA) (see Useful Addresses and Literature, page 101) has developed a widely accepted x-ray process that can often detect CHD. This test is usually used on dogs over the age of two years old, when the highest degree of certainty can be

Handling Canine Emergencies

Here are some time-tested suggestions that may lessen the severity of injuries to your poodle and you:

• Keep calm. Don't do anything to let your poodle pick up any anxiety that you may be feeling.

• Even if the injured dog is your toy poodle and longtime pet, put a muzzle on the dog. Do it gently and reassuringly. If you don't have a muzzle, devise a makeshift one from a belt, leash, scarf, or tie.

• A severely injured dog, even a trusted poodle, may be in shock or frantic; don't you become an injured party too. Take every precaution to see that your dog doesn't further injure itself, you, or some helpful friend.

• When you have the dog securely muzzled immediately attend to any bleeding (see Bleeding, page 87).

• Be very careful as you attempt to move the poodle. If at all possible, get someone to help you. Use a wide board, a small table, or whatever will serve as a secure stretcher. Again, don't handle the injured pet roughly or drop it after you have lifted it. Either action could do more damage.

• If you are alone you could use a jacket, a small throw rug, or even a tablecloth to make a slide to move the hurt animal. Be especially gentle and move very slowly.

• Call the veterinarian, or have someone else do so on your instructions. Let the clinic know the nature of the most obvious injuries and your estimated arrival time.

• Drive carefully to the veterinary clinic. Rough, fast driving could do more harm and inattentive driving could put both you and your dog under medical care or worse!

• In all your emergency actions, follow the injunction from the Hippocratic Oath, "First, do no harm!"

---

achieved. Another way of discovering CHD is through the Penn-Hip test, which some experts consider an improvement over the x-ray process. Consult your veterinarian.

Giving Your Poodle Medicine

Knowing how to give your poodle medicine is essential for all poodle owners. You should be able to administer the prescription medicines that your veterinarian recommends. Some dogs don't like medicine and will spit out pills and capsules. One common way of getting a dog to take pills is to hide them inside some favorite treat. Another way is to take a small amount of peanut butter on a small piece of bread with the pill or capsule folded inside.

A more direct way of administering pills is to open the poodle's mouth, tilt its head back a little, and place the pill as far back on the dog's tongue as possible. Then simply close the dog's mouth, talk calmly to the dog, and wait for it to swallow.

Never throw the pill or capsule into the dog's mouth or tilt its head back very far. These actions could cause the medicine to go into the windpipe instead of down the dog's throat.

Give liquid medicines in much the same way. Always take care not to tilt the head back too far as this could cause strangling. Simply pour the medicine into the pocket formed in the corner of the mouth. Tilt the head back a short way, speak in slow, reassuring terms. Rub the underside of the poodle's neck until you are certain it has swallowed the medicine.

Always follow your veterinarian's recommendations carefully about how much to administer when, and about other factors that may relate to the specific medicine. Don't undo the good of a medicine by using more or less than is recommended.

Health Areas to Watch For

Accidents

If you have done the proper preparation and taken the proper precautions to be a poodle owner, you may eliminate many potential accidents, but you cannot prevent them all, no matter how hard you try! Because you can't prevent every mishap, you should try to be as prepared as possible in case your poodle is injured (see Handling Canine Emergencies, page 86).

Heatstroke

One of the saddest and most unnecessary ways for a dog or puppy to die is from heatstroke. Many heatstrokes occur because of ignorance or neglect on behalf of the dog's owner. The most common form of this avoidable death happens when a dog is left in a parked care on a sunny day when temperatures outside reach as high as 60°F (15.6°C). The glass, metal, and insulation of the average automobile can become the natural equivalent of a convection oven in only a few minutes.

Never leave a dog in a parked car in warm weather, even if the windows are partially open. This is true even if you are just dashing into a store for a quick purchase. Something could delay you and doom your pet to a miserable death.

Clinical signs of heatstroke include a dazed, shocky look, rapid and shallow breathing, a high fever, drooling, and gums that are a bright red. Speed is crucial in this emergency. You must lower the dog's temperature as quickly as possible. Use a mixture of cool water and rubbing alcohol, if this is available. Pour this mixture, or even straight cool water, all over the dog's body. When the animal seems cooler, drive carefully to the nearest veterinarian!

Bleeding

If your pet is bleeding, the first thing to do after taking safety precautions is to find the source of the blood. When you are certain that you have the right spot, apply firm, but gentle, pressure to the wound with your hand. If the bleeding is coming from a gash or cut on an extremity (legs or tail), apply a tourniquet between the injury and the dog's heart. Be careful to loosen this tourniquet every 15 minutes. Transport the bleeding pet to the veterinarian for further attention.

Poisons

Your poodle is in your home much of the time. There are many items in the average home that can poison your pet, sometimes items that you wouldn't even recognize as dangers! Some things that can poison your poodle are probably in your home right now:

• *Chocolate* can, in sufficient amounts, kill your poodle. Don't give a dog chocolate, put boxes of it out of reach of a curious dog.

• *Antifreeze* is a killer of dogs! They seem to really like the taste of it. Don't fail to clean up spills or leaks of this product and always keep containers of antifreeze away from areas where dogs frequent.

• *Some yard and garden plants* can become killers if a puppy or a dog eats them. Landscaping favorites like azaleas, rhododendron, and even holly can bring about death. Wild plants like mistletoe, poison sumac, and poison ivy can be fatal. There are other plants that may be garden varieties or that are found in different locales. Check with the local county extension service for a list of poisonous plants that grow near where you live and avoid these plants with your dog.

unconscious, poison may be the culprit. Other clinical signs include a change in the color of the mucous membranes, vomiting, and diarrhea. Take your dog immediately to the veterinary clinic if it is exhibiting these signs.

Preventive Maintenance

Just like any other thing of importance to you, your poodle will require some preventive maintenance in order to stay good health. Some areas that will require your attention for the life of the pet are as follows:

Teeth

Dogs depend on their teeth for many functions. Unless you pay close attention to your pet's teeth, the dog will become unpleasant to be around, prone to numerous oral problems, and may be in pain that could have been prevented. While your poodle is still a young puppy, begin a regular regimen of good dental care. This usually includes taking your pet to the veterinarian twice a year but there are things that you can do yourself to enhance your poodle's dental health.

Caring for your poodle's teeth. Regular inspections of your dog's teeth will reveal most problems and abnormalities. This chore can easily be done daily. Take a moment from play, training, or just being with your poodle and look into its mouth.
• Look regularly (at least weekly) at the teeth, gums, throat, and outside areas around the mouth. You should look for tooth problems, stains on the teeth, or mouth sores. Also check for tartar and small foreign objects like wood slivers, plant awns. or bone fragments that could have been picked up through gnawing or chewing.
• Be especially aware of tartar that is not only unsightly but can cause gum disease or tooth problems.
• Start early with home cleaning of your poodle's teeth. Just like groom-

This perky white miniature looking out of a car window makes a cute photo, but in real life this could be a recipe for disaster. A poodle is still just a dog and if left unattended could jump out of the vehicle or suffer other serious injury.

• *Houseplants* such as poinsettia, jade plants, and dieffenbachia can all cause fatalities in dogs that ingest parts of these and other plants. Contact a local nursery for a complete list of the potentially killer houseplants that are found in your area.
• *Ordinary household cleaners, insecticides, pesticides, fertilizers,* and *cleaning solvents* can all do great harm to a poodle. Store all these and other household chemicals in safe places away from where you keep your poodle. Clean up chemical spills promptly and thoroughly.

If your dog suddenly has convulsions, becomes listless, disoriented, or is

ing, training, and other areas of poodle ownership, the earlier you establish an activity as a regular part of the dog's life, the easier it will be.

• To clean your dog's teeth, use veterinarian-approved brushes, utensils, and toothpaste designed for dogs *not humans!* Try tooth brushing daily for best results, but never less than two or three times each week.

• Tartar scraping is an unpleasant chore that only gets worse if you neglect to do it. Consult your veterinarian about how often your poodle will need your services as a tartar remover. Severe tartar buildup will probably require your veterinarian's skill.

• A number of chew toys are designed to help stimulate the gums and keep tartar to a minimum. While these items may assist you, no toy, biscuit, chew, or bone will do the job you can do with regular care.

This handsome silver has been bred, raised, trained, and carefully groomed just for appearing in the show ring. This miniature is in a show pose that gives the dog show judge the best look possible at the poodle. What happens next is up to the judge.

Eyes

Your poodle's eyes are among its most beautiful assets. Eye care is another lifelong task that you must assume when you decide to become a responsible dog owner. Poodles are active and can sometimes put themselves in danger of eye injuries. You will need to become a canine risk manager and help your poodle avoid potentially blinding injuries.

• Wherever you go with your poodle or wherever your poodle is allowed to go in your home, be diligent about removing sharp, eye-level things that could harm an exuberant poodle's eyes. Your poodle might not see the sharp wires, the rosebush thorns, or any of a myriad or potential eye-damaging things. You must try to make your pet's environment as safe as possible.

• Caution children about throwing stones, playing with air rifles, or doing anything around your poodle that could endanger its eyes.

• Protect your poodle from eye harm caused by chemicals. Avoid fumes or residue that could get into a dog's eyes and irritate them.

• Never let your poodle ride in the car with its head out of the window. It only takes a piece of road debris, or even a large insect to hurt a pet's eyes at the highway speed of the average car.

• Check your dog's eyes on a daily basis for injuries, irritation, infection, foreign objects, or similar problems. Don't confuse infection with the mucous that will sometimes collect in the corner of a dog's eye. This harmless mucous can be easily removed with a soft, slightly damp cloth.

Ears

Your poodle's ears should be checked as often as you should check its teeth or eyes—daily! The inside part of the ears of the poodle are not readily visible as they are in some other breeds. Take extra care to seek out this favorite hiding place for ear mites and ticks. Look for injuries or infections. Don't let small children put foreign objects in a dog's ears. Poodles also grow hair in their ears that must be plucked out before it mats and causes blockage and infection.

Feet and Toenails

In some places where poodles live there is hard stone, concrete, or asphalt to wear down the dog's toenails as it runs. It is true that running under these conditions can keep nails worn down where they won't need much trimming but it is also true that such surfaces can cause bruises, abrasions, and wear on the pads of a dog's feet. Salt and other chemicals that can be found on city streets, parking lots, and sidewalks can also irritate or harm a dog's feet.

A poodle that spends all of its life inside or inside with access to a grassy backyard will not have the foot pad problems of the urban dog running on paved roads, but neither will its nails be worn away. Toenails will have to be

It is important when trimming your poodle's nails to avoid hitting the vein in the toenail, commonly called the quick.

trimmed. As with other aspects of grooming, the earlier such activities are introduced to the dog, the better.

Trimming the nails: You will need a good set of nail trimmers designed for dogs. These can be either the "scissors" type or the "guillotine" type. As your poodle's nails grow, snip them back by trimming just the tips of each nail. Don't trim too much of the nail off or you will hit the vein in the nail called the *quick,* which may bleed. If you are unsure how much nail is too much, use an emery board instead of nail clippers. You are less likely to injury the vein in the nail that way. After trimming, smooth the edges of the nail with an emery board or nail file. If you paint your poodle's nails, be certain that the polish you use is safe if the dog should gnaw some off.

As Your Poodle Grows Older

Poodles generally have long life spans. That adorable puppy may be with you for a decade and a half. Your children can grow up with one poodle under ideal genetic and environmental circumstances. How you treat, feed, and care for the dog will have an impact on its life span and the quality of that life span. For example, if you persist in feeding table scraps and the dog becomes obese, it probably will not live the same number of years it would have on a healthy, balanced diet.

Eventually, whatever you do, the toddling puppy will make way for the bouncy adolescent. This canine teenager will move over to allow the adult to take center stage. The adult will gradually age into a dignified, but still spritely senior. Seniority will begin well, but ever so gradually your beloved poodle will slow down.

Old dogs sleep a little more and play a little less, but they will still relish the quiet times near you and your family. The good care you gave the poodle in earlier years will now start to pay extra dividends because its nails, teeth, eyes, ears, and general health will have been attended to all along.

Your old poodle will still show flashes of that spunky puppy that you came to love. It will still want to patrol its guard posts to make certain your household is secure. It will still need lots of tender, loving, care. Your poodle may become a more frequent visitor at its old friend's, the veterinarian's. As long as an old dog remains reasonably healthy, don't take away its little chores and duties. Try not to upset its routine. Don't be harsh with an oldster that is doing the best it can with slowed reflexes and bodily functions that just won't wait sometimes. Repay the poodle in the same currency that it has rewarded you all its life—with love.

Euthanasia

This is never an easy subject to plan for, to discuss, or even to contemplate, but there may come a time when your poodle's existence is only one of pain and suffering. The aging process has continued and the valiant old dog has handled it the very best that it could, but age always wins. It will be up to you to see that your poodle's losing fight against age isn't a painful, prolonged, unnecessary last, lost battle.

Unless your poodle is killed in an accident, dies early of some ailment, or dies naturally, it will live a long life that will possibly leave you with one of the most difficult decisions a dog owner can ever have to make—how much suffering is too much?

Barring an early death, one day your poodle will look up at you in a questioning manner, wanting you to take the pains away, wanting you to make things the way they used to be, wanting you to set things right. You have to make a tough, adult decision. Does this good dog, one that has loved you with all of its considerable poodle heart, deserve to go on in a pained or incapacitated state? Your veterinarian can help you with this decision and the timing of it, but only you can truly know when it is finally best to say good-bye.

Breeding Poodles

Poodles have been popular for a long time. That they even exist today only speaks well for their resilient nature and the disciplined devotion of dedicated, knowledgeable poodle fans. There have been countless instances of overbreeding in this breed, but a strong breed club like the Poodle Club of America has worked to decrease overbreeding. The Poodle Club of America has a foundation dedicated to research into the wide variety of physical ailments and defects that plague poodles, especially in puppy-assembly-line breeding and haphazard backyard breeding situations. The PCA has also instituted a variety of educational and awareness-building programs that help breeders and owners understand their responsibilities to the breed.

Rescuing Poodles

The Poodle Club of America Rescue Central (see Useful Addresses and Literature, page 101) spends many thousands of dollars each year to save poodles that have been abandoned by their owners, turned over to animal shelters or dog pounds, or that have problems that otherwise may deprive them of their homes and families. Not only are there thousands of poodle puppies born that shouldn't be, but many adult poodles are in need of caring, poodle-knowledgeable families. Your decision to breed your average poodle will almost certainly add to the overabundance of poodles we already have. Why not contact PCA Rescue

Central and find a good adult poodle in need of a good home?

Even with the best efforts of the breed club, poodles have continued to suffer because of their popularity. Poodles, as a breed, have quite a number of genetically transmitted ailments. Some dogs, called poodles and registered as poodles, are not poodles at all; they are mere imitations of the genuine article, impostors in poodle coats that do great disservice to the real breed! Unscrupulous "breeders" crank out these "poodles" in amazingly large numbers for the often gullible, ill-informed, impulse-driven puppy buyer.

Should You Breed Your Poodle?

No, you shouldn't. Just in case that answer wasn't clear enough, the answer is "**No**." If simply purchasing a poodle is an investment, breeding your poodle should be considered a major undertaking. There are so many potential problems for you, your poodle, and the people who may obtain any poodle puppies you cause to be born that the odds are overwhelmingly against your poodle producing anything that can have a lasting, positive impact on the breed.

Unless your poodle is a top-quality show specimen with strong obedience trial potential, why would you want to perpetuate what is probably just a pet-quality dog? Loving your pet-quality poodle is admirable; wanting to reproduce more pet-quality dogs is not. Even the top poodle breeders in the country, breeding the best poodles available to them, will produce relatively few excellent poodles. Many of the pups born in even the best of kennels will be end up as family pets.

Dog breeding is an intricate, time-consuming, and often frustrating endeavor. The financial rewards are nonexistent if one factors in all the time that must be spent, medical expenses, and other variables. The top poodle breeders in the United States may make some money, but for each dog breeder who makes any profit, there are several thousand or more who make nothing!

Most reputable poodle breeders are so aware of ill-suited people trying to breed poodles that it may not even be possible for an average beginner to purchase a good brood bitch or stud dog at *any* price. Respectable dog breeders strive to protect the poodle as a breed, and their own individual poodles, from the "breed-for-greed" exploitation seen so often in popular breeds. Until you prove yourself to be a sincere dog breeder interested in, and capable of, producing poodles of excellent quality, you may receive the "cold shoulder." If you fit that mold, you will respect this attitude and come to hold it yourself at some point if you eventually become a breeder of quality poodles.

Taking a Hard Look at Raising Poodles

Causing a litter of poodle puppies to be born should always be a very serious decision. Casual breeding of any dogs, without regard for the future of the resultant pups, is irresponsible in the best light and animal abuse in the worst.

Those cute poodle puppies grow up to be adult dogs. They deserve every chance to be a part of a household that really cares for them in a competent way. The acid test for a truly responsible dog breeder is whether

that person is willing to keep for life each and every puppy that he or she allows to be born. If you aren't willing to make this pledge: "If necessary, I will keep every puppy that I breed for its entire life!" then you shouldn't contemplate raising poodles.

The Brood Bitch

Looking through magazines on dogs and dog breeding, one sees that there is a great deal of emphasis placed on stud dogs. This is as it should be, but certainly not in any way should the quality, disposition, health, and genetic stability of the brood bitch be left to chance. If you have chosen a female poodle puppy from an excellent line of quality poodles, if she is sound in temperament and health, if she has been critically approved as possible breeding stock by acknowledged poodle experts—especially if she has been successfully campaigned to her AKC show championship and has an obedience title—you *may* have a brood bitch candidate.

The Right Age for Breeding

Most breed experts agree that your poodle bitch should be at least two

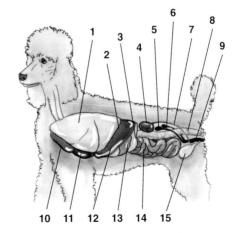

The internal organs of the female poodle.

1. Lung
2. Diaphragm
3. Spleen
4. Kidney
5. Ovary
6. Uterine Horn
7. Ureter
8. Colon
9. Vagina
10. Thymus
11. Heart
12. Liver
13. Stomach
14. Jejunum
15. Bladder

93

years old and have received her OFA evaluation prior to her first breeding. You will also have enough time for her to have been exposed to show ring and/or obedience trial competition.

The Stud Dog

As with your poodle female, the choice of a poodle male to sire a litter of puppies must be based on the qualities of disposition, health, quality, and compatibility. Since it is practically impossible for you, as a first-time poodle owner, to have obtained a male poodle of true stud potential, the choice of a stud dog belonging to someone else is your only course of action.

Excellence in health, disposition, and quality is just as important in the stud dog as it is in the brood bitch. If the male you have chosen to sire your bitch's puppies is deficient in any of these areas, find another stud dog. If you can't find another stud, have your bitch spayed and forget breeding.

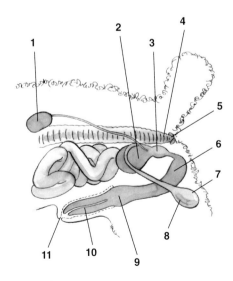

1. Kidneys
2. Bladder
3. Prostrate
4. Rectum
5. Anus
6. Urethra
7. Scrotum
8. Testes
9. Bulb
10. Penis
11. Sheath

The reproductive system of the male poodle.

The Estrous Cycle

Female dogs will usually come into heat, or season, two times each year, each of which can last up to three weeks. Your poodle female's first heat will probably occur sometime between six and eight months of age. Some poodles may be ahead of that time line and others a bit behind it, but on average this is about the right age for a first heat. Of course, just because a poodle bitch comes into season doesn't mean that she should be bred. Her first season merely means that her reproductive system has matured to the point where she is able to have puppies.

The cyclical phases of what happens, or can happen, when a female canine comes into season is called the *estrous cycle*. There are several stages within the estrous cycle and which stages occur will depend on whether your female becomes pregnant or not.

Proestrus: The first stage of the estrous cycle is called *proestrus*. It can be recognized by the initial activity that takes place within the uterus and the ovaries. Ova, or eggs, begin to be produced by the ovaries. As the ova mature, the walls of the uterus will become thicker and a blood-colored vaginal discharge is observable. The outer genitalia, the vulva, will appear somewhat larger than usual during this time.

Proestrus will usually continue for about nine days, although it may last as few as four days or as long as two weeks. Your female poodle will attract male dogs during the proestrus stage, but she will not be ready to mate with them. Many owners of unspayed poodle females will use sanitary belts and pads and similar devices to protect clothing and furniture from staining from vaginal fluids during and after proestrus.

Estrus: The next stage in the estrous cycle is *estrus*. (Remember that estrous is the cycle and estrus is just one phase or stage of this cycle.) The vaginal discharge during estrus often loses the bloody tinge and becomes clearer, thinner, and more mucouslike. Male dogs will continue to be attracted and special care must be taken during estrus that unintended matings do not take place.

Ovulation occurs during estrus and will normally happen between the ninth and fourteenth day after the start of the proestrus part of the estrous cycle. Estrus will normally last about as long as proestrus did. Conception can take place during the entire nine or so days of estrus following proestrus.

Metestrus (or diestrus): If your poodle bitch has mated during the estrus phase, the next phase of metestrus will soon begin and will continue for the next six to eight weeks. This stage is recognized by the onset of physical changes in your poodle preparing her mammary glands for lactation or milk production. (This is also the cycle phase when all false pregnancies occur in unspayed females.)

Anestrus: The end of the metestrus phase or stage of the estrous cycle ushers in anestrus. Anestrus marks the return of the bitch's body back to its condition before the estrous cycle began. If your poodle did not mate and conceive, she will gradually return to her "pre-season" form: Her vulva will shrink; vaginal discharge should cease; her ovaries will become dormant until her next time to go into heat approximately six months in the future when the whole estrous cycle starts again!

Warning: During the entire estrous cycle you would be wise to keep your in-season poodle away from unneutered male dogs of any age, any physical condition, and any size. Because you may not be absolutely certain when proestrus goes into estrus (when mating can take place),

you should be especially careful to protect your poodle bitch from her mating instincts and an unwanted litter.

Mating

Most dog breeders try to put the stud dog with the ovulating female on the ninth day of the estrus stage of the estrous cycle. Care should be taken not to simply put two poodles together and let nature take its course. If your female is a virgin, she may have some difficulty or even hostility during the act toward the stud. You want to protect both animals at this time. If you have chosen a proven poodle stud dog, its owner or handler should be there to oversee the mating. You may want an experienced poodle breeder friend to be along with you.

When copulation between two dogs occurs, the dogs will usually become "tied" or locked together. This is a very natural effect of the interaction between the male's penis and the female's vagina and should subside in 10 to 20 minutes. It is possible that a male and female poodle could mate and even become "tied" more than once during the two or so days of maximum receptiveness. *Remember that your poodle could mate again with a different dog and cast serious doubts about the actual parentage of the resultant litter.* Prevent this from happening by keeping her away all other males during this entire time!

False Pregnancy

False pregnancy can occur when an unspayed poodle female fails to conceive after mating, or even if she was not involved with mating at all. This condition—false pregnancy—can be the result of high progesterone or the presence of ovarian cysts. There are veterinary treatments to help with false pregnancy, but a bitch can develop pyometritis and other related ailments that could result in a need for surgery.

Note: The vast majority of wonderful, loving female poodles that find their way into homes as companions and pets do not need to be perceived as breeding stock. False pregnancy and other conditions will not affect your dog if she is spayed. Spaying is definitely in her best interest if she is not one of that tiny minority that deserves to be bred. You will be relieved of the problems associated with the estrous cycle and the possibility of unwanted litters and your female poodle will be relieved of many health-threatening matters. Everyone—human and poodle—wins!

Pregnancy

Under most circumstances, the canine gestation period (the time it takes puppies to develop) is 63 days after the mating. At about the sixth week of gestation your poodle bitch will begin to take on the look and feel of a matron. Her abdomen will get larger. Her teats will grow in order to feed her hungry poodle pups. Treat

One of the most important aspects of a well constructed whelping box is that it has a safety shelf all around the inside perimeter of the box to keep a mother dog from unintentionally smothering or crushing one of the puppies.

your poodle kindly at all times, but especially now. If this is her first litter she may be fretful at the changes happening to her. Be aware and very understanding at this trying time.

It is important that weight gain in pregnant bitches be from the fast-growing puppies and not from fat. A fat poodle bitch may have some whelping (birthing) difficulties. Feed her a highly nutritious diet (possibly the same food you will be feeding her puppies in a few weeks) to help make healthy pups and keep her in good health. Give her regular physical activity, but don't overdo it.

Fourteen or fifteen days before the date you have marked down as 63 days after the mating, you will be wise to separate the pregnant female from other dogs you may have. She should also be safeguarded from overly enthusiastic children and from any physically strenuous or stressful situations. Handle her with care now. Avoid any rough play or fast running that might injure her. Let her have ready access to her cage/crate/carrier denning area. Keep her quiet, and see to her emotional and physical needs. This is even more important if she is in whelp with her first litter.

Preparations for Whelping

You may want to schedule your veterinarian to be on standby and perhaps your poodle mentor/friend to be in attendance in case of complications when whelping time does arrive. As whelping day nears, your brood bitch may become restless. Always be very gentle and tender with her. Keep stress and confusion out of her life as much as you can. Spend time with her during her pregnancy; many poodles are quite sensitive to any perceived lack of attention. Show her that she may be going through strange physical changes but that your love for her has not changed.

This poodle mother is contently nursing her two pups. Raising poodles is a risky situation that novices should best leave to reputable breeders with decades of experience.

If you are feeling a little stressed out about the coming birth day, talk things over with your poodle-mentor and the veterinarian. You might try reading some of the more in-depth books on whelping and newborn care. Don't just believe you *know* what to do, know what to do! Most poodles are good mothers, but you must not become complacent now and turn everything over to a first-time poodle mom. Be there for moral support and in case you are needed to help her.

The Whelping Box

Follow the old Boy Scout motto to the hilt: Be Prepared. Don't wait until the puppies are due before you start getting ready for them. One major preparation need is the whelping box. This important birthing location is essential for the well-being and easy care of your soon-to-arrive puppies.

There are many diagrams on how to construct a whelping box, but you may be wise to avail yourself of one of the new collapsible boxes available through most quality pet products retailers. You should be able to get a box made of coated, heavy-duty cardboard or fiberboard of a size appropriate for the size poodle you have: toy, miniature, or standard. Whether you buy one of these inexpensive manufactured boxes or make one yourself, the whelping box should be large enough for your poodle bitch to lie down comfortably, stretched out on her side. This is crucial because the whelping box is not only the delivery room for your new poodles, it will also be their nursery for the first few weeks of their lives.

The whelping box should be placed in a warm, dry place. Keep the box away from drafts and out of heavily traveled areas. On the floor of the whelping box put several layers of black-and-white newspapers. Avoid newspapers with colored pictures or printing because of the chemicals sometimes used in such colored printing. Plain, blank newsprint is even better. As the puppies make messes in the whelping box, simply lift the soiled layer and dispose of it. Using this approach will make cleaning the box easier and also keep disruption of the whelping box to a minimum.

Note: A very important aspect in any whelping box is a protective shelf that will prevent a puppy from being caught between its mother's body and the side of the box. Without this shelf puppies can be crushed or smothered accidentally by their mothers.

The Whelping Kit

Consult with your more experienced poodle friends and with your veterinarian about the things you may need to have nearby during whelping. If you assemble such a kit well in advance of the scheduled whelping, you won't get caught off balance if the puppies arrive a little early. Include the following items in your whelping kit (and any others mentioned by your veterinarian and poodle-mentors):

• A current telephone roster containing the phone numbers (and beeper numbers) of your veterinarian and your poodle-mentor.

• Heavy surgical thread, or dental floss, and a pair of sharp-edged, sterilized scissors to use for first tying off and then cutting the umbilical cords.

• Clean, absorbent, soft towels for drying off the new poodles.

• A towel-lined heat box, with a heating pad wrapped in a towel and on a low setting, to keep early arrivals warm (not hot) while their siblings are still being born.

• A note pad so that you can mark down observations about which puppy came first and so forth. While toys

generally have quite small litters, miniatures and standards can have fairly large ones.

• In the possibility that your poodle will not have maternal interest in any of her puppies after they are born, have a puppy-feeding bottle and some of the milk replacer formula (available at most better pet products retailers) ready for use.

• The last ingredient in your whelping kit is a liberal amount of good judgment. Stay calm. Move slowly around your poodle. Don't excite her or do anything to distract her at this important time. Build on the sense of tender loving care that you have kept strong in recent days and weeks.

Whelping

Since you have studied and learned about the whelping process you know that the mother dog will usually pull away the birth sac and chew through the umbilical cord of each puppy as it is born. If she doesn't do this you can assist her by tying off and cutting the cord.

Your poodle mother will clean each newborn by licking it gently and by nosing it toward her milk-laden teats. This first meal, loaded with health-giving colostrum, is very important. Colostrum lets a puppy share its mother's immunity to many diseases (she should have had all her shots long before whelping. This immunity is only temporary, but it gives the baby poodles just that much more chance at surviving.).

If the baby can't find its way or the mother is concerned with the next pup, you can help. Moving slowly and deliberately, place the newborn puppy up against its mother's teats. Always speak slowly and calmly to the mother so she knows that her new baby is safe. As the birthing continues, place the baby poodle in the heated box to keep it warm, making sure you don't upset its mother in the process.

After each puppy is whelped, some afterbirth should come out. Mother dogs generally eat this afterbirth. Veterinary opinions vary on the value of this instinctual behavior, but many believe that the mother actually is able to somewhat replenish hormones and other elements that she has lost in the whelping process. In any opinion, the brood bitch's eating of afterbirth is a natural occurrence that shouldn't trouble you. You should be concerned if, after the last newborn appears, the last of the afterbirth doesn't come out. If you believe that this is the case, call your veterinarian.

Puppy Care

The room where the whelping box is placed should be kept consistently at temperatures between 80 and 85°F (26.7–29.4°C). Newborn puppies cannot tolerate severe variations in temperature. Their mother will try to keep them warm. Her thick poodle coat should help, but you can and should keep the temperature in the proper range much more easily than she can.

By the time these new poodle puppies are three days old, the veterinarian can dock their tails and have their dewclaws removed. *Insist* that your veterinarian follow your instructions and dock (cut off) only one-third of each puppy's tail. More or less than one-third and the puppy's appearance is ruined!

If your mother dog dies or can't or won't care for her puppies, these tasks will fall to you. As their foster mother you will be required to feed them, a job that must be done each and every four hours for the first month of their lives! Feeding them will become an all-encompassing role for you or some other responsible family member. One poodle owner, faced with just such a situation, took her motherless puppies with her to her place of work and was allowed to use break times to give the youngsters their meals of veterinarian-approved milk replacer.

When your poodles are six weeks old they will need their first temporary immunization shots. Your veterinarian, who has already seen these youngsters to dock their tails, can also worm them at this time. Though growing rapidly, these little poodles are still too young to leave home and Mama.

Weaning

Your poodle bitch will know when to wean her offspring. You can assist her in this by gradually introducing puppy food to the pups while they are still nursing. Start with the best available dry puppy food. Moisten this food to make it damp, but not soggy. Let this softened dry puppy food get all over your fingertips and let the baby poodles smell this intriguing new scent. They can begin solid food by licking very small morsels off your fingers. Don't rush them. Gradually make lightly moistened puppy food available to them, being sure to have fresh water nearby.

When feeding a litter of hungry poodle puppies, use a sturdy feeding pan with a flat bottom to avoid upsets that will mess up the whelping box. Allow the mother dog a chance to go outside to the backyard or to another room so that she won't compete with the puppies for the solid food. Gradually feed more and more solid food as the mother dog begins the weaning process. Weaning, which can be traumatic to the babies, will go much easier if they have already been introduced to solid, but easily digestible food. Always follow the puppy feeding rule of never changing foods!

Finding Good Homes for the Puppies

Now that you are the breeder you will find your role reversed. Instead of being the seeker of a quality poodle puppy, you are now the seeker of a

A couple taking their two poodles out for a walk, or perhaps it is the other way around. Both dogs are securely attached to a leash for absolute safety.

quality home for your quality poodle puppy. Think back to all the questions your dog's breeder asked you. Remember the lessons you learned in trying to convince this breeder that you would provide good care and a good home. Let the buyers of your litter (those puppies that don't belong to your co-owner or that you want to keep for yourself) be the way you were when you sincerely wanted a good poodle youngster to take home with you. Put your thinking in reverse and follow the steps you've learned about finding the right poodle puppy backward toward the goal of acting as a responsible breeder seeking the best possible homes for his/her puppies.

Two pals from the American Kennel Club's Toy Group, a Pomeranian (left) and a silver toy poodle. The toy poodle is a much younger breed than the standard and the miniature.

Useful Addresses and Literature

Organizations

American Kennel Club
  51 Madison Avenue
  New York, New York 10038
  (212) 696-8200

AKC Registration and Information
  5580 Centerview Drive, Suite 200
  Raleigh, North Carolina 27606-3390
  (919) 233-9767

Charles Thomasson, Secretary
  Poodle Club of America
  503 Martineau Drive
  Chester, Virginia 23831
  (804) 530-1605

Helen Taylor
  Poodle Club of America Rescue
  Central
  3912 Rice Boulevard
  Houston, Texas 77005
  (713) 668-1021

Jody Wahlig
  Poodle Club of America Foundation
  2945 Jamestown Road
  Long Lake, Minnesota 55356

Canadian Kennel Club
  89 Skyway Avenue
  Etobicoke, Ontario
  Canada M9W 6R4

American Boarding Kennel Association
  4575 Galley Road, Suite 400A
  Colorado Springs, Colorado 80915

Orthopedic Foundation for Animals
  2300 Nifong Boulevard
  Columbia, Missouri 65201
  (314) 442-0418

Genetic Disease Control Registry
  P.O. Box 222
  Davis, California 95617
  (916) 756-6773

Magazines

Dog World
  29 North Wacker Drive
  Chicago, Illinois 60606-3298
  (312) 726-2802

Dog Fancy
  P.O. Box 53264
  Boulder, Colorado 80322-3264
  (303) 666-8504

The Poodle Review
  Holfin Publishing
  4401 Zepher Street
  Wheat Ridge, Colorado 80033

The Poodle Variety
  P.O. Box 30430
  Santa Barbara, California 93130

Books

Alderton, David. *The Dog Care Manual*. Hauppauge, New York: Barron's Educational Series, Inc. 1986.

Baer, Ted. *Communicating With Your Dog*. Hauppauge, New York: Barron's Educational Series, Inc. 1989.

Brown, Robert M. *The Poodle Owner's Medical Manual.* Jackson, Wisconsin: Breed Manual Publications. 1987.

Dahl, Del. *The Complete Poodle.* New York, New York: Howell Book House. 1994.

Kalstone, Shirlee. *The Complete Poodle Clipping and Grooming Book.* New York, New York: Howell Book House. 1981.

Wrede, Barbara. *Civilizing Your Puppy.* Hauppauge, New York: Barron's Educational Series, Inc. 1992.

Video

Poodle #VVT701
   The American Kennel Club
   Attn: Video Fulfillment
   5580 Centerview Drive, Suite 200
   Raleigh, North Carolina 27606

Further Reading on Poodles
Steinbeck, John. *Travels With Charley.* New York, New York: The Viking Press, Inc. 1962.

Berenson, Laurien. *A Pedigree To Die For.* New York, New York: Kensington Publishing Corp. 1995.

Index